TEFAL EASY FRY AIR FRYER &GRILL COOKBOOK UK

The Ultimate Guide of Delicious Air Fryer Recipes With Healthy and Juicy Meals for Beginners & Advanced Users in the UK

CYNTHIA .S. MEDINA

Copyright© 2024 By CYNTHIA .S. MEDINA. Allrights reservedworldwide.

No part of this book may be reproduced or transmittedinany form or by any means, electronic or mechanical, including photocopying, recording, or by any informations to rage and retrieval system, without written permission from the publisher, except for the inclusion of brief quotations in are view.

Warning-Disclaimer:

The purpose of this book is to educate and entertain. The author or publisher does not guarantee that anyone following the techniques, suggestions, tips, ideas, or strategies will become successful. The author and publisher shall have neither liability nor responsibility to anyone with respect to any loss or damage caused, or all eged to becaused, directly or indirectly, by the information contained in this book.

This copy right notice and disclaimer apply to the entirety of the book and its contents, whether in print or electronic form, and extend to all future editions or revisions of the book. Unauthorized use or reproduction of this book or its contents is strictly prohibited and may result in legal action.

TABLE OF CONTENTS

INTRODUCTION 6

CHAPTER 1 Appetizers and Snacks 10

Air-Fried Chicken Wings with Honey Garlic Sauce 10
Grilled Veggie Skewers with Balsamic Glaze 11
Crispy Air-Fried Chickpeas 11
Grilled Halloumi Bites with Mint and Lemon 12
Air-Fried Jalapeño Poppers 13
Grilled Bruschetta with Tomato and Basil 13
Air-Fried Zucchini Chips 14
Grilled Stuffed Mushrooms 15
Air-Fried Cauliflower Bites with Ranch Dip 15
Grilled Pineapple Skewers with Lime Zest 16

CHAPTER 2 Breakfast and Brunch 17

Air-Fried Avocado Toast with Poached Eggs 17
Grilled Veggie Frittata 18
Air-Fried Hash Browns 18
Grilled Breakfast Burrito with Scrambled Eggs and Chorizo 19
Air-Fried French Toast Sticks with Berry Compote 20
Grilled Tomato and Basil Bruschetta 20
Air-Fried Breakfast Potatoes 21
Grilled Bagel Sandwiches with Cream Cheese and Smoked Salmon 21
Air-Fried Cinnamon Rolls 22
Grilled Stuffed Avocados with Eggs and Bacon 22

CHAPTER 3 Poultry Dishes 24

.Air-Fried Chicken Parmesan 24
Grilled Lemon Herb Chicken Breasts 25

Air-Fried Turkey Meatballs with Marinara Sauce 25
Grilled Chicken Fajitas 26
Air-Fried Crispy Chicken Tenders 26
Grilled Teriyaki Chicken Skewers 27
Air-Fried Buffalo Cauliflower Wings 27
Grilled Moroccan Chicken Thighs 28
Air-Fried Chicken Drumsticks with Honey Mustard Glaze 29
Grilled Chicken Caesar Salad 29

CHAPTER 4 Beef and Pork Dishes 31

Air-Fried Steak Fajitas 31
Grilled Pork Chops with Apple Chutney 31
Air-Fried Beef Meatballs with Sweet and Sour Sauce 32
Grilled Beef Burgers with Caramelized Onions 33
Air-Fried Beef Empanadas 33
Grilled Pork Tenderloin with Chimichurri Sauce 34
Air-Fried Beef Kofta Kebabs 34
Grilled BBQ Pulled Pork Sandwiches 35
Air-Fried Beef and Vegetable Skewers 35
Grilled Pork Belly Bites with Honey Soy Glaze 36

CHAPTER 5 Seafood Dishes 37

Air-Fried Coconut Shrimp with Sweet Chili Sauce 37
Grilled Salmon with Mango Salsa 37
Air-Fried Fish Tacos with Cabbage Slaw 38
Grilled Shrimp Skewers with Garlic Butter 39
Air-Fried Crispy Calamari Rings 39
Grilled Tuna Steaks with Mediterranean Salsa 40
Air-Fried Crab Cakes with Remoulade Sauce 40
Grilled Swordfish Skewers with Pineapple Salsa 41
Air-Fried Fish and Chips 41
Grilled Lobster Tails with Garlic Butter 42

CHAPTER 6 Vegetarian and Vegan Dishes 43

- Air-Fried Falafel with Tahini Sauce 43
- Grilled Portobello Mushroom Burgers with Caramelized Onions 44
- Air-Fried Tofu Bites with Teriyaki Glaze 44
- Grilled Veggie Kebabs with Balsamic Marinade 45
- Air-Fried Cauliflower Steaks with Romesco Sauce 45
- Grilled Eggplant Parmesan 46
- Air-Fried Chickpea Fritters with Tzatziki Sauce 47
- Grilled Stuffed Bell Peppers with Quinoa and Vegetables 47
- Air-Fried Vegetable Samosas with Mint Chutney 48
- Grilled Vegan Lentil Burgers 48

CHAPTER 7 Side Dishes 50

- Air-Fried Roasted Potatoes with Rosemary and Garlic 50
- Grilled Asparagus with Lemon Garlic Butter 50
- Air-Fried Zucchini Fries 51
- Grilled Corn on the Cob with Chili Lime Butter 51
- Air-Fried Sweet Potato Wedges with Chipotle Mayo 52
- Grilled Balsamic Roasted Brussels Sprouts 52
- Air-Fried Parmesan Roasted Green Beans 53
- Grilled Hasselback Potatoes with Crispy Bacon 53
- Air-Fried Carrot Fries with Honey Mustard Dip 54
- Grilled Garlic Butter Mushrooms 55

CHAPTER 8 Sandwiches and Wraps 56

- Air-Fried Chicken Wraps with Tzatziki Sauce 56
- Grilled Veggie Panini with Pesto Aioli 56
- Air-Fried Falafel Wraps with Tahini Sauce 57
- Grilled Philly Cheesesteak Sandwiches 58
- Air-Fried BLT Wraps 58
- Grilled Caprese Sandwiches 59

- Air-Fried Crispy Tofu Banh Mi Sandwiches ... 59
- Grilled Chicken Caesar Wraps ... 60
- Air-Fried Buffalo Chicken Wraps ... 60
- Grilled Portobello Mushroom Sandwiches ... 61

CHAPTER 9 Desserts and Sweet Treats ... 62

- Air-Fried Churros with Chocolate Sauce ... 62
- Grilled Peaches with Honey Yogurt ... 62
- Air-Fried Apple Fritters ... 63
- Grilled Pineapple Skewers with Coconut Caramel Sauce ... 63
- Air-Fried Baked Apples with Cinnamon and Walnuts ... 64
- Grilled Banana Boats with Chocolate and Marshmallows ... 64
- Air-Fried Donuts with Assorted Glazes ... 65
- Grilled Strawberry Shortcake Skewers ... 66
- Air-Fried Cinnamon Sugar Pretzel Bites ... 66
- Grilled Coconut Lime Bars ... 67

CHAPTER 10 Bonus Recipes and Tips ... 68

- Air-Fried Nachos with Pulled Pork and Guacamole ... 68
- Grilled Pizza with Assorted Toppings ... 68
- Air-Fried Doughnuts with Raspberry Glaze ... 69
- Grilled Flatbread with Baba Ghanoush and Feta ... 69
- Air-Fried Crispy Tofu Bites with Sriracha Mayo ... 70
- Grilled Panzanella Salad with Grilled Bread ... 71
- Air-Fried Potato Skins with Bacon and Cheddar ... 71
- Grilled Vegetable Pasta Salad ... 72
- Air-Fried Blooming Onion with Dipping Sauce ... 72
- Grilled Fruit Skewers with Honey Lime Glaze ... 73

Conclusion ... 75

INTRODUCTION

What is an Air Fryer?

An Tefal air fryer is a revolutionary kitchen appliance that has taken the world by storm in recent years. It's a compact countertop oven that uses rapid air circulation and a powerful heating element to "fry" foods with little to no oil. But don't let the name deceive you - it's so much more than just a fryer!

When I first heard about air fryers, I was a bit skeptical. How could this small appliance achieve the same crispy, delicious results as traditional deep frying without all the oil and mess? But after trying it out for myself, I was instantly converted.

An Tefal air fryer is essentially a miniature convection oven that mimics the flow of hot air around the food, similar to what you'd find in a commercial-grade kitchen. The key difference is that the air fryer's compact design and powerful fan allow for much more intense heat circulation, resulting in that irresistible crispy texture we all crave.

I'll never forget the first time I made french fries in my air fryer. I was amazed at how crispy and golden they came out, with only a light misting of oil. And the cleanup was a breeze compared to the splattery mess of deep frying.

How Air Fryers Work

The magic behind air fryers lies in their unique design and cooking process. At the core of every Tefal air fryer is a heating element and a powerful fan. When you turn on the appliance, the heating element generates intense heat, and the fan rapidly circulates that hot air around the food placed in the fryer basket or tray.

This constant circulation of hot air creates a crispy, crunchy exterior on your food, much like deep frying, but without the need for submerging it in oil. The Tefal air fryer essentially "fries" the outside of your food while baking the inside to perfection.

What really sold me on the Tefal air fryer was how versatile it is. Sure, you can make crispy fries, wings, and other typical fried foods. But air fryers can also bake, roast, reheat, and dehydrate a wide variety of dishes. I've made everything from tender chicken breasts to flaky fish fillets, roasted veggies, baked pastries, and more!

The rapid air circulation ensures even cooking on all sides, so you don't have to flip or rotate the food as often as with conventional ovens. Plus, the Tefal air fryer preheats in just 2-3 minutes, making it super convenient for quick meals or snacks.

With its space-saving design, easy cleaning, and incredible versatility, it's no wonder air fryers have become a kitchen staple for busy households. Whether you're looking to cut down on oil and calories or just want deliciously crispy meals with little effort, an Tefal air fryer is a game-changer.

Benefits of Air Frying (Healthier, Faster, Convenient)

One of the biggest selling points of air fryers is that they allow you to enjoy your favorite fried foods in a much healthier way. When I was relying on traditional frying methods, I knew it was doing no favors for my waistline or my overall health. Submerging foods in vats of scorching hot oil loads them up with excessive fat, calories, and a host of other unhealthy stuff.

With an air fryer, you can achieve that crispy, crave-worthy texture by using just a small amount of oil or even none at all. Most recipes call for only a light misting or brushing of oil onto the foods before air frying. This simple switch instantly cuts down on so much fat and calories compared to deep frying. I felt better knowing I could indulge in foods like fries, chicken wings, and crispy fish fillets without drowning them in oil first.

Beyond just reducing fat and calories, air frying is a healthier cooking method because none of the potentially toxic byproducts are created that can occur when foods are submerged in extremely hot oil for prolonged periods. There's no risk of acrylamides forming or nutrients being transferred away into the oil. The high heat still creates that perfect crispy texture, but in a much safer way.

Another huge benefit is just how fast and convenient air fryers are to use. These mighty little appliances can preheat and have food cooking in under 3 minutes in most cases. Comparing that to firing up the big oven or waiting for a pot of oil to heat up, and you've just saved yourself 15-20 minutes of time right from the start.

The speed of air fryers doesn't stop at the preheating phase either. Most foods cook in anywhere from 8-25 minutes depending on what you're making. I've had entire meals, including crispy protein and roasted veggies, ready to serve in under 30 minutes thanks to my air fryer. It's a total game-changer for getting delicious food on the table quickly without having to rely on unhealthy shortcuts or deliveries.

Air fryers are also incredibly convenient and easy to use, with minimal monitoring required during the cooking process. The rapid air circulation cooks food extremely evenly, so you rarely have to stop and flip, rotate, or shuffle the ingredients around like you would in an oven. I can literally set the temp and timer, walk away, and my food comes out perfect every time.

Speaking of convenience, the compact size of air fryers makes them a ideal fit for apartments, RVs, dorms, or any kitchen with limited counter space. You can easily stash it away in a cabinet or corner when not in use. And unlike fryers filled with scorching oil, air fryers are super safe to use around children. The outer surfaces stay cool to the touch, and any splattering of oil inside is very minimal compared to traditional frying methods.

With so many health, speed, and convenience factors going for them, it's no surprise that air fryers have earned a permanent spot in millions of kitchens around the world. They really do combine all the great things we love about fried foods without the negatives. If you've been on the fence about getting one, I highly recommend taking the plunge!

Introduction to Air Frying and Grilling

In recent years, air frying and grilling have become popular cooking methods for those seeking a healthier and more convenient way to prepare delicious meals. As someone who has embraced this culinary revolution, I can attest to the incredible versatility and ease that these techniques offer. Whether you're looking to indulge in crispy fried delights or savor the smoky flavors of grilled dishes, the Tefal Easy Fry Air Fryer & Grill is a game-changer in the world of home cooking.

But what exactly is an air fryer, you might ask? Well, let me break it down for you. An air fryer is a compact countertop appliance that uses rapid air circulation and a small amount of oil to mimic the crispiness and texture of deep-fried foods. It's like having a miniature convection oven that can transform ordinary ingredients into crispy perfection with just a fraction of the oil traditionally used in deep frying.

The magic lies in the combination of hot air and a small amount of oil, which creates a delightfully crispy outer layer while keeping the inside moist and tender. Say goodbye to the greasy mess and lingering odors of traditional frying, and hello to a healthier and more convenient cooking experience.

But that's not all - the Tefal Easy Fry Air Fryer & Grill also doubles as a versatile grill, allowing you to achieve those coveted charred and smoky flavors without the hassle of firing up an outdoor grill. With its specialized grill plate and adjustable temperature settings, you can sear meats, fish, and vegetables to perfection, infusing them with a delicious grilled taste right in the comfort of your kitchen.

One of the greatest benefits of air frying and grilling is the ability to create delicious, crispy, and flavorful dishes without compromising on health. By using minimal oil and relying on hot air circulation or direct grilling, you can significantly reduce the amount of fat and calories in your meals, making it easier to maintain a balanced and nutritious diet.

Imagine being able to indulge in crispy chicken wings, perfectly grilled steaks, or even decadent desserts without the guilt or the added pounds. With the Tefal Easy Fry Air Fryer & Grill, you can have your cake and eat it too - literally!

But beyond the health benefits, air frying and grilling offer unparalleled convenience and versatility in the kitchen. Gone are the days of standing over a hot stove, constantly flipping and monitoring your food. With the Tefal Easy Fry Air Fryer & Grill, you can simply pop in your ingredients, set the timer, and let the appliance work its magic, freeing you up to focus on other tasks or simply relax while your meal cooks to perfection.

Whether you're a seasoned home chef or a culinary novice, the Tefal Easy Fry Air Fryer & Grill is designed to make your life easier and your meals more enjoyable. Its user-friendly interface, easy-to-clean design, and compact size make it a perfect addition to any modern kitchen, catering to both busy families and singles alike.

In the pages of this cookbook, we'll dive deeper into the world of air frying and grilling, exploring a wide array of delicious and family-friendly recipes that showcase the versatility of this remarkable appliance. From crispy appetizers and snacks to mouth-watering main courses and indulgent desserts, you'll discover a world of flavors and textures that will tantalize your taste buds and leave you craving for more.

So, whether you're a health-conscious foodie, a busy parent seeking convenient meal solutions, or simply someone who appreciates good food and innovative cooking techniques, the Tefal Easy Fry Air Fryer & Grill Cookbook UK is your ultimate guide to mastering this revolutionary cooking method. Get ready to embark on a culinary adventure that will transform the way you think about healthy and delicious meals – one crispy, grilled bite at a time!

CHAPTER 1 APPETIZERS AND SNACKS

Air-Fried Chicken Wings with Honey Garlic Sauce

Prep: 10mins | Cook: 25mins | Serves: 4

Ingredients:

- UK: 1kg chicken wings, 30ml olive oil, 2 teaspoons garlic powder, 1 teaspoon salt, 1 teaspoon black pepper, 60ml honey, 3 cloves garlic (minced), 30ml soy sauce, 1 tablespoon butter

Instructions:

1. Preheat your Tefal Easy Fry Air Fryer to 180°C (350°F).
2. Toss the chicken wings in a bowl with olive oil, garlic powder, salt, and pepper until evenly coated.
3. Arrange the wings in a single layer in the air fryer basket.
4. Cook for 25 minutes, shaking the basket halfway through to ensure even cooking.
5. Prepare the sauce: In a small saucepan, combine honey, minced garlic, soy sauce, and butter. Heat over medium heat until the butter is melted and the sauce is smooth.
6. Toss the cooked wings in the honey garlic sauce until well coated.
7. Serve hot, garnished with chopped spring onions if desired.

Grilled Veggie Skewers with Balsamic Glaze

Prep: 15mins | Cook: 10mins | Serves: 4

Ingredients:

- UK: 2 bell peppers (cut into chunks), 1 red onion (cut into chunks), 2 courgettes (sliced), 250g cherry tomatoes, 60ml olive oil, 30ml balsamic vinegar, 1 teaspoon dried oregano, salt, pepper

Instructions:

1. Preheat your Tefal Easy Fry Air Fryer & Grill to 200°C (390°F).
2. Skewer the vegetables, alternating colours and types for a visually appealing presentation.
3. Mix olive oil, balsamic vinegar, dried oregano, salt, and pepper in a small bowl.
4. Brush the skewers with the balsamic mixture.
5. Grill the skewers for about 10 minutes, turning occasionally, until the veggies are tender and slightly charred.
6. Serve immediately as a vibrant and healthy starter or side dish.

Crispy Air-Fried Chickpeas

Prep: 5mins | Cook: 20mins | Serves: 4

Ingredients:

- UK: 400g canned chickpeas (drained and rinsed), 30ml olive oil, 1 teaspoon paprika, 1 teaspoon garlic powder, 1/2 teaspoon salt, 1/2 teaspoon black pepper

Instructions:

1. Preheat your Tefal Easy Fry Air Fryer to 200°C (390°F).
2. Pat dry the chickpeas with a paper towel to remove excess moisture.
3. Toss the chickpeas with olive oil, paprika, garlic powder, salt, and pepper in a bowl.
4. Spread the chickpeas in the air fryer basket in a single layer.
5. Air fry for 20 minutes, shaking the basket halfway through, until crispy and golden brown.
6. Cool slightly before serving as a crunchy snack or salad topper.

Grilled Halloumi Bites with Mint and Lemon

Prep: 10 mins | Cook: 10 mins | Serves: 4

Ingredients:

- UK: 250g halloumi cheese (cut into cubes), 30ml olive oil, juice of 1 lemon, 1 tablespoon fresh mint (chopped), black pepper

Instructions:

1. 1. Preheat your Tefal Easy Fry Air Fryer & Grill to 200°C (390°F).
2. 2. Mix olive oil, lemon juice, chopped mint, and black pepper in a bowl.
3. 3. Toss the halloumi cubes in the lemon and mint mixture.
4. 4. Grill the halloumi in the air fryer for about 10 minutes, turning halfway, until golden and slightly crispy.
5. 5. Serve immediately, garnished with extra mint leaves if desired.

Air-Fried Jalapeño Poppers

Prep: 15 mins | Cook: 10 mins | Serves: 4

Ingredients:

- UK: 8 large jalapeños, 100g cream cheese, 50g cheddar cheese (grated), 1 teaspoon garlic powder, 1 teaspoon onion powder, 30g panko breadcrumbs, 1 egg (beaten)

Instructions:

1. 1. Preheat your Tefal Easy Fry Air Fryer to 180°C (350°F).
2. 2. Halve the jalapeños lengthwise and remove the seeds and membranes.
3. 3. Mix cream cheese, grated cheddar, garlic powder, and onion powder in a bowl until well combined.
4. 4. Fill each jalapeño half with the cheese mixture.
5. 5. Dip the filled jalapeños in the beaten egg, then coat with panko breadcrumbs.
6. 6. Arrange the poppers in the air fryer basket.
7. 7. Air fry for 10 minutes, until the breadcrumbs are golden and crispy.
8. 8. Serve hot, with a dipping sauce of your choice.

Grilled Bruschetta with Tomato and Basil

Prep: 10 mins | Cook: 5 mins | Serves: 4

Ingredients:

- UK: 4 slices of ciabatta bread, 2 large tomatoes (diced), 2 tablespoons olive oil, 1 garlic clove (minced), 1 tablespoon balsamic vinegar, 10 fresh basil leaves (chopped), salt, pepper

Instructions:

1. 1. Preheat your Tefal Easy Fry Air Fryer & Grill to 200°C (390°F).
2. 2. Toast the ciabatta slices in the air fryer for about 5 minutes, until golden and crispy.
3. 3. Mix diced tomatoes, olive oil, minced garlic, balsamic vinegar, chopped basil, salt, and pepper in a bowl.
4. 4. Top each slice of toasted ciabatta with the tomato mixture.
5. 5. Serve immediately as a fresh and flavourful appetizer.

Air-Fried Zucchini Chips

Prep: 10mins | Cook: 15mins | Serves: 4

Ingredients:

- UK: 2 medium courgettes, 60g panko breadcrumbs, 30g grated Parmesan cheese, 1 teaspoon garlic powder, 1 teaspoon dried oregano, 1 egg (beaten), salt, pepper

Instructions:

1. Preheat your Tefal Easy Fry Air Fryer to 200°C (390°F).
2. Slice the zucchinis into thin rounds.
3. Mix panko breadcrumbs, grated Parmesan, garlic powder, and dried oregano in a bowl.
4. Dip each zucchini slice into the beaten egg, then coat with the breadcrumb mixture.
5. Arrange the zucchini slices in a single layer in the air fryer basket.
6. Air fry for 15 minutes, shaking the basket halfway through, until crispy and golden.
7. Serve hot as a healthy snack or side dish.

Grilled Stuffed Mushrooms

Prep: 15 mins | Cook: 10 mins | Serves: 4

Ingredients:

- UK: 8 large mushrooms, 100g cream cheese, 50g spinach (chopped), 2 garlic cloves (minced), 30g grated Parmesan cheese, 1 tablespoon olive oil, salt, pepper

Instructions:

1. Preheat your Tefal Easy Fry Air Fryer & Grill to 200°C (390°F).
2. Remove the stems from the mushrooms and set aside.
3. Mix cream cheese, chopped spinach, minced garlic, and grated Parmesan in a bowl until well combined.
4. Fill each mushroom cap with the cream cheese mixture.
5. Brush the filled mushrooms with olive oil.
6. Grill the mushrooms in the air fryer for about 10 minutes, until tender and golden.
7. Serve hot as a tasty appetizer.

Air-Fried Cauliflower Bites with Ranch Dip

Prep: 10 mins | Cook: 20 mins | Serves: 4

Ingredients:

- UK: 1 medium cauliflower (cut into florets), 60g panko breadcrumbs, 30g grated Parmesan cheese, 1 teaspoon garlic powder, 1 teaspoon paprika, 1 egg (beaten), salt, pepper

Instructions:

1. Preheat your Tefal Easy Fry Air Fryer to 200°C (390°F).
2. Mix panko breadcrumbs, grated Parmesan, garlic powder, and paprika in a bowl.
3. Dip each cauliflower floret into the beaten egg, then coat with the breadcrumb mixture.
4. Arrange the cauliflower florets in a single layer in the air fryer basket.
5. Air fry for 20 minutes, shaking the basket halfway through, until crispy and golden.
6. Serve hot with a side of ranch dip.

Grilled Pineapple Skewers with Lime Zest

Prep: 10mins | Cook: 10mins | Serves: 4

Ingredients:

- UK: 1 pineapple (cut into chunks), 30ml honey, zest of 1 lime, 1 teaspoon ground cinnamon

Instructions:

1. Preheat your Tefal Easy Fry Air Fryer & Grill to 200°C (390°F).
2. Thread the pineapple chunks onto skewers.
3. Mix honey, lime zest, and ground cinnamon in a bowl.
4. Brush the pineapple skewers with the honey mixture.
5. Grill the pineapple skewers in the air fryer for about 10 minutes, turning halfway, until caramelised and golden.
6. Serve hot as a sweet and tangy snack or dessert.

CHAPTER 2 BREAKFAST AND BRUNCH

Air-Fried Avocado Toast with Poached Eggs

Prep: 10 mins | Cook: 15 mins | Serves: 2

Ingredients:

- UK: 2 avocados (sliced), 4 slices of wholegrain bread, 2 eggs, 1 tablespoon olive oil, 1 teaspoon chilli flakes, salt, pepper, 1 tablespoon fresh chives (chopped)

Instructions:

1. Preheat your Tefal Easy Fry Air Fryer to 180°C (350°F).
2. Brush the bread slices with olive oil and place them in the air fryer basket.
3. Air fry the bread for about 5 minutes until golden and crispy.
4. Poach the eggs in a saucepan with boiling water for about 3 minutes, until the whites are set and the yolks are still runny.
5. Mash the avocado slices and spread them onto the toasted bread.
6. Top each toast with a poached egg.
7. Sprinkle with chilli flakes, salt, pepper, and chopped chives.
8. Serve immediately for a healthy and delicious breakfast.

GrilledVeggieFrittata

Prep:15mins|Cook:20mins|Serves:4

Ingredients:

- UK: 6 eggs, 100ml milk, 1 red bell pepper (diced), 1 green bell pepper (diced), 1 small onion (diced), 100g cherry tomatoes (halved), 50g spinach (chopped), 50g grated cheddar cheese, salt, pepper, 1 tablespoon olive oil

Instructions:

1. Preheat your Tefal Easy Fry Air Fryer & Grill to 180°C (350°F).
2. Whisk together the eggs, milk, salt, and pepper in a large bowl.
3. Heat the olive oil in a non-stick pan over medium heat. Add the diced bell peppers, onion, and cherry tomatoes. Cook for 5 minutes until softened.
4. Add the spinach to the pan and cook for another 2 minutes until wilted.
5. Pour the egg mixture over the vegetables and cook for 2 minutes until the edges start to set.
6. Sprinkle grated cheddar cheese on top.
7. Transfer the pan to the air fryer and cook for 10-12 minutes until the frittata is set and golden.
8. Serve hot or at room temperature, cut into wedges.

Air-FriedHashBrowns

Prep:10mins|Cook:20mins|Serves:4

Ingredients:

- UK: 500g potatoes (peeled and grated), 1 small onion (grated), 1 egg, 2 tablespoons plain flour, 1 teaspoon salt, 1/2 teaspoon black pepper, 2 tablespoons olive oil

Instructions:

1. Preheat your Tefal Easy Fry Air Fryer to 200°C (390°F).
2. Squeeze excess moisture from the grated potatoes and onion using a clean tea towel.
3. Combine the grated potatoes and onion in a bowl with the egg, flour, salt, and pepper.

4. Form the mixture into small patties.
5. Brush the patties with olive oil on both sides.
6. Place the patties in the air fryer basket in a single layer.
7. Air fry for 20 minutes, flipping halfway through, until golden and crispy.
8. Serve hot with your favourite breakfast sides.

Grilled Breakfast Burrito with Scrambled Eggs and Chorizo

Prep: 10 mins | Cook: 15 mins | Serves: 4

Ingredients:

- UK: 4 large flour tortillas, 200g chorizo (sliced), 6 eggs, 100ml milk, 1 red bell pepper (diced), 1 small onion (diced), 50g grated cheddar cheese, 2 tablespoons olive oil, salt, pepper

Instructions:

1. Preheat your Tefal Easy Fry Air Fryer & Grill to 200°C (390°F).
2. Cook the chorizo in a pan over medium heat until crispy. Remove and set aside.
3. In the same pan, add olive oil and cook the diced bell pepper and onion until softened.
4. Whisk together the eggs, milk, salt, and pepper. Pour into the pan with the vegetables and cook, stirring, until the eggs are scrambled and cooked through.
5. Warm the tortillas in the air fryer for 1 minute.
6. Assemble the burritos: Place scrambled eggs, chorizo, and grated cheese in the centre of each tortilla. Fold and roll them up.
7. Grill the burritos in the air fryer for 5 minutes until the tortillas are golden and crispy.
8. Serve hot with your favourite salsa or hot sauce.

Air-Fried French Toast Sticks with Berry Compote

Prep: 10 mins | Cook: 15 mins | Serves: 4

Ingredients:

- UK: 8 slices of thick white bread, 3 eggs, 100ml milk, 1 teaspoon vanilla extract, 1 teaspoon ground cinnamon, 50g butter (melted), 200g mixed berries, 2 tablespoons sugar, 1 tablespoon lemon juice

Instructions:

1. Preheat your Tefal EasyFry Air Fryer to 180°C (350°F).
2. Cut each slice of bread into three sticks.
3. Whisk together the eggs, milk, vanilla extract, and ground cinnamon in a shallow dish.
4. Dip each breadstick into the egg mixture, ensuring they are fully coated.
5. Arrange the breadsticks in the air fryer basket in a single layer.
6. Air fry for 10-15 minutes, turning halfway through, until golden and crispy.
7. While the toast cooks, prepare the berry compote: In a small saucepan, combine mixed berries, sugar, and lemon juice. Cook over medium heat until the berries are soft and the mixture thickens.
8. Serve the French toast sticks hot with the berry compote.

Grilled Tomato and Basil Bruschetta

Prep: 10 mins | Cook: 5 mins | Serves: 4

Ingredients:

- UK: 4 slices of ciabatta bread, 2 large tomatoes (diced), 2 tablespoons olive oil, 1 garlic clove (minced), 1 tablespoon balsamic vinegar, 10 fresh basil leaves (chopped), salt, pepper

Instructions:

1. Preheat your Tefal EasyFry Air Fryer & Grill to 200°C (390°F).
2. Toast the ciabatta slices in the air fryer for about 5 minutes, until golden and crispy.
3. Mix diced tomatoes, olive oil, minced garlic, balsamic vinegar, chopped basil, salt, and pepper in a bowl.
4. Top each slice of toasted ciabatta with the tomato mixture.

5. Serve immediately as a fresh and flavourful breakfast or brunch dish.

Air-Fried Breakfast Potatoes

Prep: 10 mins | Cook: 20 mins | Serves: 4

Ingredients:

- UK: 500g baby potatoes (quartered), 1 tablespoon olive oil, 1 teaspoon paprika, 1 teaspoon garlic powder, salt, pepper, 1 tablespoon fresh parsley (chopped)

Instructions:

1. Preheat your Tefal Easy Fry Air Fryer to 200°C (390°F).
2. Toss the quartered potatoes with olive oil, paprika, garlic powder, salt, and pepper.
3. Arrange the potatoes in a single layer in the air fryer basket.
4. Air fry for 20 minutes, shaking the basket halfway through, until the potatoes are golden and crispy.
5. Garnish with chopped fresh parsley before serving.
6. Serve hot as a hearty breakfast side dish.

Grilled Bagel Sandwiches with Cream Cheese and Smoked Salmon

Prep: 10 mins | Cook: 5 mins | Serves: 2

Ingredients:

- UK: 2 bagels (halved), 100g cream cheese, 100g smoked salmon, 1 small red onion (thinly sliced), 1 tablespoon capers, 1 tablespoon fresh dill (chopped), 1 teaspoon lemon juice

Instructions:

1. Preheat your Tefal Easy Fry Air Fryer & Grill to 200°C (390°F).
2. Toast the bagel halves in the air fryer for about 5 minutes, until golden and crispy.
3. Spread cream cheese evenly on each toasted bagel half.
4. Top with smoked salmon, thinly sliced red onion, capers, and chopped dill.
5. Drizzle with lemon juice.

6. 6. Serve immediately for a quick and delicious breakfast or brunch.

Air-Fried Cinnamon Rolls

Prep: 20mins | Cook: 15mins | Serves: 6

Ingredients:

- UK: 250g plain flour, 7g instant yeast, 50g sugar, 125ml warm milk, 50g butter (melted), 1 egg, 1 teaspoon ground cinnamon, 100g brown sugar, 50g butter (softened), 100g cream cheese, 50g icing sugar, 1 teaspoon vanilla extract

Instructions:

1. 1. Preheat your Tefal Easy Fry Air Fryer to 180°C (350°F).
2. 2. In a bowl, combine flour, instant yeast, and sugar. Add warm milk, melted butter, and egg. Mix until a dough forms.
3. 3. Knead the dough on a floured surface for about 5 minutes until smooth and elastic.
4. 4. Roll the dough into a rectangle.
5. 5. Spread softened butter over the dough and sprinkle with ground cinnamon and brown sugar.
6. 6. Roll the dough tightly into a log and cut into 6 even pieces.
7. 7. Place the rolls in the air fryer basket, leaving space between them.
8. 8. Air fry for 15 minutes until golden and cooked through.
9. 9. While the rolls cook, prepare the icing: Mix cream cheese, icing sugar, and vanilla extract until smooth.
10. 10. Drizzle the icing over the warm cinnamon rolls.
11. 11. Serve immediately for a sweet and indulgent treat.

Grilled Stuffed Avocados with Eggs and Bacon

Prep: 10mins | Cook: 15mins | Serves: 4

Ingredients:

- UK: 2 large avocados (halved and pitted), 4 eggs, 4 strips of bacon (cooked and crumbled), 50g grated cheddar cheese, 1 tablespoon fresh chives (chopped), salt, pepper

Instructions:

1. 1. Preheat your Tefal EasyFry Air Fryer & Grill to 200°C (390°F).
2. 2. Scoop out a bit more of the avocado flesh to make room for the egg.
3. 3. Crack an egg into each avocado half.
4. 4. Season with salt and pepper.
5. 5. Place the stuffed avocados in the air fryer basket.
6. 6. Air fry for about 10-15 minutes until the eggs are cooked to your liking.
7. 7. Top with crumbled bacon, grated cheddar cheese, and chopped chives.
8. 8. Serve hot as a nutritious and filling breakfast.

CHAPTER 3 POULTRY DISHES

Air-Fried Chicken Parmesan

Prep: 15mins | Cook: 20mins | Serves: 4

Ingredients:

- UK: 4 chicken breasts (about 500g), 100g breadcrumbs, 50g grated Parmesan cheese, 1 egg (beaten), 200ml marinara sauce, 100g mozzarella cheese (sliced), 30ml olive oil, salt, pepper, 1 tablespoon fresh basil (chopped)

Instructions:

1. Preheat your Tefal Easy Fry Air Fryer to 200°C (390°F).
2. Mix the breadcrumbs and grated Parmesan cheese in a shallow bowl.
3. Dip each chicken breast in the beaten egg, then coat with the breadcrumb mixture.
4. Arrange the chicken breasts in the air fryer basket in a single layer.
5. Spray or brush the tops with olive oil.
6. Air fry for 15 minutes, turning halfway through, until the chicken is golden and cooked through.
7. Top each chicken breast with marinara sauce and a slice of mozzarella cheese.
8. Return to the air fryer and cook for an additional 3-5 minutes until the cheese is melted and bubbly.
9. Garnish with chopped fresh basil.
10. Serve hot with a side of pasta or salad.

Grilled Lemon Herb Chicken Breasts

Prep: 10 mins | Cook: 15 mins | Serves: 4

Ingredients:

- UK: 4 chicken breasts (about 500g), 50ml lemon juice, 30ml olive oil, 2 cloves garlic (minced), 1 tablespoon fresh thyme (chopped), 1 tablespoon fresh rosemary (chopped), salt, pepper

Instructions:

1. Preheat your Tefal Easy Fry Air Fryer & Grill to 200°C (390°F).
2. In a bowl, mix lemon juice, olive oil, minced garlic, chopped thyme, and rosemary.
3. Season the chicken breasts with salt and pepper.
4. Marinate the chicken in the lemon herb mixture for at least 10 minutes.
5. Place the chicken breasts on the grill plate.
6. Grill for 15 minutes, flipping halfway through, until the chicken is cooked through and has grill marks.
7. Serve hot with your favourite sides.

Air-Fried Turkey Meatballs with Marinara Sauce

Prep: 15 mins | Cook: 15 mins | Serves: 4

Ingredients:

- UK: 500g ground turkey, 50g breadcrumbs, 1 egg, 2 cloves garlic (minced), 30g grated Parmesan cheese, 1 tablespoon fresh parsley (chopped), 200ml marinara sauce, salt, pepper

Instructions:

1. Preheat your Tefal Easy Fry Air Fryer to 200°C (390°F).
2. In a bowl, mix ground turkey, breadcrumbs, egg, minced garlic, grated Parmesan, chopped parsley, salt, and pepper until well combined.
3. Form the mixture into small meatballs.
4. Arrange the meatballs in the air fryer basket in a single layer.

5. Air fry for 12-15 minutes, shaking the basket halfway through, until the meatballs are browned and cooked through.
6. Heat the marinara sauce in a small saucepan.
7. Serve the meatballs topped with warm marinara sauce.

Grilled Chicken Fajitas

Prep: 15mins | Cook: 15mins | Serves: 4

Ingredients:

- UK: 500g chicken breasts (sliced into strips), 1 red bell pepper (sliced), 1 yellow bell pepper (sliced), 1 green bell pepper (sliced), 1 large onion (sliced), 30ml olive oil, 1 tablespoon fajita seasoning, tortillas, sour cream, salsa, lime wedges

Instructions:

1. Preheat your Tefal Easy Fry Air Fryer & Grill to 200°C (390°F).
2. In a bowl, toss the chicken strips, bell peppers, and onion with olive oil and fajita seasoning.
3. Place the mixture on the grill plate in a single layer.
4. Grill for 15 minutes, stirring halfway through, until the chicken is cooked through and the vegetables are tender.
5. Serve with warm tortillas, sour cream, salsa, and lime wedges.

Air-Fried Crispy Chicken Tenders

Prep: 10mins | Cook: 12mins | Serves: 4

Ingredients:

- UK: 500g chicken tenders, 100g breadcrumbs, 50g flour, 2 eggs (beaten), 1 teaspoon paprika, 1 teaspoon garlic powder, salt, pepper, 30ml olive oil

Instructions:

1. Preheat your Tefal Easy Fry Air Fryer to 200°C (390°F).
2. In a bowl, mix breadcrumbs, paprika, garlic powder, salt, and pepper.

3. Coat the chicken tenders in flour, dip in beaten eggs, then coat with the breadcrumb mixture.
4. Arrange the chicken tenders in the air fryer basket in a single layer.
5. Spray or brush the tops with olive oil.
6. Air fry for 10-12 minutes, turning halfway through, until golden and crispy.
7. Serve with your favourite dipping sauce.

Grilled Teriyaki Chicken Skewers

Prep: 20 mins | Cook: 10 mins | Serves: 4

Ingredients:

- UK: 500g chicken breasts (cut into chunks), 50ml teriyaki sauce, 1 red bell pepper (cut into chunks), 1 green bell pepper (cut into chunks), 1 red onion (cut into chunks), 2 tablespoons sesame seeds, 1 tablespoon fresh coriander (chopped)

Instructions:

1. Preheat your Tefal EasyFry Air Fryer & Grill to 200°C (390°F).
2. In a bowl, marinate the chicken chunks in teriyaki sauce for at least 15 minutes.
3. Thread the marinated chicken, bell peppers, and red onion onto skewers.
4. Place the skewers on the grill plate.
5. Grill for 10 minutes, turning halfway through, until the chicken is cooked through and has grill marks.
6. Sprinkle with sesame seeds and chopped coriander.
7. Serve hot with steamed rice or salad.

Air-Fried Buffalo Cauliflower Wings

Prep: 10 mins | Cook: 15 mins | Serves: 4

Ingredients:

- UK: 1 large cauliflower (cut into florets), 50g flour, 2 eggs (beaten), 100ml buffalo sauce, 30g butter (melted), 1 tablespoon fresh chives (chopped)

Instructions:

1. Preheat your Tefal EasyFry Air Fryer to 200°C (390°F).
2. Coat the cauliflower florets in flour, dip in beaten eggs, then coat with buffalo sauce.
3. Arrange the cauliflower in the air fryer basket in a single layer.
4. Air fry for 15 minutes, shaking the basket halfway through, until crispy and golden.
5. Toss the cooked cauliflower in melted butter mixed with more buffalo sauce.
6. Garnish with chopped fresh chives.
7. Serve hot with a side of blue cheese dressing.

Grilled Moroccan Chicken Thighs

Prep: 15mins | Cook: 20mins | Serves: 4

Ingredients:

- ❖ UK: 500g chicken thighs, 50ml olive oil, 1 tablespoon ground cumin, 1 tablespoon ground coriander, 1 teaspoon ground cinnamon, 1 teaspoon ground ginger, 2 cloves garlic (minced), salt, pepper, 1 tablespoon fresh coriander (chopped)

Instructions:

1. Preheat your Tefal EasyFry Air Fryer & Grill to 200°C (390°F).
2. In a bowl, mix olive oil, ground cumin, ground coriander, ground cinnamon, ground ginger, minced garlic, salt, and pepper.
3. Marinate the chicken thighs in the spice mixture for at least 15 minutes.
4. Place the marinated chicken thighs on the grill plate.
5. Grill for 20 minutes, flipping halfway through, until the chicken is cooked through and has grill marks.
6. Garnish with chopped fresh coriander.
7. Serve hot with couscous or salad.

Air-Fried Chicken Drumsticks with Honey Mustard Glaze

Prep: 10 mins | Cook: 25 mins | Serves: 4

Ingredients:

- UK: 8 chicken drumsticks (about 500g), 50ml honey, 50ml Dijon mustard, 1 tablespoon olive oil, salt, pepper, 1 tablespoon fresh parsley (chopped)

Instructions:

1. Preheat your Tefal Easy Fry Air Fryer to 200°C (390°F).
2. In a bowl, mix honey, Dijon mustard, olive oil, salt, and pepper.
3. Coat the chicken drumsticks with the honey mustard mixture.
4. Arrange the drumsticks in the air fryer basket in a single layer.
5. Air fry for 25 minutes, turning halfway through, until the drumsticks are golden and cooked through.
6. Garnish with chopped fresh parsley.
7. Serve hot with a side of coleslaw or potato salad.

Grilled Chicken Caesar Salad

Prep: 10 mins | Cook: 15 mins | Serves: 4

Ingredients:

- UK: 2 chicken breasts (about 500g), 30ml olive oil, 1 teaspoon garlic powder, salt, pepper, 1 large romaine lettuce (chopped), 50g Parmesan cheese (shaved), 100g croutons, 100ml Caesar dressing, 1 tablespoon fresh parsley (chopped)

Instructions:

1. Preheat your Tefal Easy Fry Air Fryer & Grill to 200°C (390°F).
2. In a bowl, coat the chicken breasts with olive oil, garlic powder, salt, and pepper.
3. Place the chicken breasts on the grill plate.
4. Grill for 15 minutes, flipping halfway through, until the chicken is cooked through and has grill marks.
5. Slice the grilled chicken into strips.
6. In a large bowl, toss chopped romaine lettuce with Caesar dressing.

7. 7.Topwithgrilledchickenstrips,shavedParmesancheese,andcroutons.
8. 8.Garnishwithchoppedfreshparsley.
9. 9.Serveimmediately.

CHAPTER 4 BEEF AND PORK DISHES

Air-Fried Steak Fajitas

Prep: 15 mins | Cook: 15 mins | Serves: 4

Ingredients:

- UK: 500g steak (sliced into strips), 1 red bell pepper (sliced), 1 green bell pepper (sliced), 1 large onion (sliced), 30ml olive oil, 1 tablespoon fajita seasoning, tortillas, sour cream, salsa, lime wedges

Instructions:

1. Preheat your Tefal Easy Fry Air Fryer to 200°C (390°F).
2. In a bowl, toss the steak strips, bell peppers, and onion with olive oil and fajita seasoning.
3. Place the mixture in the air fryer basket in a single layer.
4. Air fry for 15 minutes, shaking the basket halfway through, until the steak is cooked through and the vegetables are tender.
5. Serve with warm tortillas, sour cream, salsa, and lime wedges.

Grilled Pork Chops with Apple Chutney

Prep: 15 mins | Cook: 20 mins | Serves: 4

Ingredients:

- UK: 4 pork chops (about 600g), 30ml olive oil, salt, pepper, 2 apples (peeled and chopped), 1 onion (chopped), 30g brown sugar, 30ml apple cider vinegar, 1 teaspoon ground cinnamon

Instructions:

1. Preheat your Tefal Easy Fry Air Fryer & Grill to 200°C (390°F).
2. Season the pork chops with salt and pepper, and brush with olive oil.
3. Place the pork chops on the grill plate.

4. 4. Grill for 15-20 minutes, flipping halfway through, until the pork chops are cooked through and have grill marks.
5. 5. Meanwhile, in a saucepan, cook the apples, onion, brown sugar, apple cider vinegar, and ground cinnamon over medium heat until the apples are tender and the mixture has thickened.
6. 6. Serve the grilled pork chops with a generous spoonful of apple chutney on top.

Air-Fried Beef Meatballs with Sweet and Sour Sauce

Prep: 15mins | Cook: 15mins | Serves: 4

Ingredients:

- ❖ UK: 500g ground beef, 50g breadcrumbs, 1 egg, 2 cloves garlic (minced), 30g grated Parmesan cheese, 1 tablespoon fresh parsley (chopped), 100ml sweet and sour sauce, salt, pepper

Instructions:

1. 1. Preheat your Tefal Easy Fry Air Fryer to 200°C (390°F).
2. 2. In a bowl, mix ground beef, breadcrumbs, egg, minced garlic, grated Parmesan, chopped parsley, salt, and pepper until well combined.
3. 3. Form the mixture into small meatballs.
4. 4. Arrange the meatballs in the air fryer basket in a single layer.
5. 5. Air fry for 12-15 minutes, shaking the basket halfway through, until the meatballs are browned and cooked through.
6. 6. Heat the sweet and sour sauce in a small saucepan.
7. 7. Serve the meatballs topped with warm sweet and sour sauce.

Grilled Beef Burgers with Caramelized Onions

Prep: 15 mins | Cook: 15 mins | Serves: 4

Ingredients:

- UK: 500g ground beef, 1 egg, 30g breadcrumbs, 1 onion (sliced), 30ml olive oil, 4 burger buns, lettuce, tomato, cheese slices, salt, pepper

Instructions:

1. Preheat your Tefal Easy Fry Air Fryer & Grill to 200°C (390°F).
2. In a bowl, mix ground beef, egg, breadcrumbs, salt, and pepper. Form into burger patties.
3. Place the burger patties on the grill plate.
4. Grill for 12-15 minutes, flipping halfway through, until the burgers are cooked through and have grill marks.
5. Meanwhile, heat olive oil in a pan and cook the sliced onions over medium heat until caramelized.
6. Assemble the burgers with lettuce, tomato, cheese slices, and caramelized onions in burger buns.
7. Serve hot with your favourite sides.

Air-Fried Beef Empanadas

Prep: 20 mins | Cook: 15 mins | Serves: 4

Ingredients:

- UK: 500g ground beef, 1 onion (chopped), 2 cloves garlic (minced), 1 red bell pepper (chopped), 100g olives (sliced), 1 teaspoon cumin, 1 teaspoon paprika, 200g puff pastry, 1 egg (beaten), salt, pepper

Instructions:

1. Preheat your Tefal Easy Fry Air Fryer to 200°C (390°F).
2. In a pan, cook the ground beef, chopped onion, minced garlic, and red bell pepper until the beef is browned and the vegetables are tender.
3. Stir in the sliced olives, cumin, paprika, salt, and pepper. Let the mixture cool.
4. Roll out the puff pastry and cut into circles. Place a spoonful of the beef mixture on each circle.
5. Fold the pastry over to form empanadas, sealing the edges with a fork. Brush with beaten egg.
6. Arrange the empanadas in the air fryer basket in a single layer.

7. Air fry for 12-15 minutes until golden and crispy.
8. Serve hot with your favourite dipping sauce.

Grilled Pork Tenderloin with Chimichurri Sauce

Prep: 15 mins | Cook: 20 mins | Serves: 4

Ingredients:

- UK: 500g pork tenderloin, 30ml olive oil, 1 teaspoon garlic powder, 1 teaspoon paprika, salt, pepper, 50ml chimichurri sauce

Instructions:

1. Preheat your Tefal Easy Fry Air Fryer & Grill to 200°C (390°F).
2. Coat the pork tenderloin with olive oil, garlic powder, paprika, salt, and pepper.
3. Place the pork tenderloin on the grill plate.
4. Grill for 20 minutes, turning halfway through, until the pork is cooked through and has grill marks.
5. Slice the pork tenderloin and serve with chimichurri sauce on the side.

Air-Fried Beef Kofta Kebabs

Prep: 20 mins | Cook: 15 mins | Serves: 4

Ingredients:

- UK: 500g ground beef, 1 onion (grated), 2 cloves garlic (minced), 1 teaspoon ground cumin, 1 teaspoon ground coriander, 1 teaspoon ground paprika, salt, pepper, 30ml olive oil, fresh parsley (chopped, for garnish)

Instructions:

1. Preheat your Tefal Easy Fry Air Fryer to 200°C (390°F).
2. In a bowl, mix ground beef, grated onion, minced garlic, ground cumin, ground coriander, ground paprika, salt, and pepper until well combined.
3. Form the mixture into kebabs around skewers.

4. 4. Brush the kebabs with olive oil.
5. 5. Place the kebabs in the air fryer basket in a single layer.
6. 6. Air fry for 12-15 minutes, turning halfway through, until the kebabs are cooked through and browned.
7. 7. Serve garnished with chopped fresh parsley.

Grilled BBQ Pulled Pork Sandwiches

Prep: 15 mins | Cook: 3 hours | Serves: 4

Ingredients:

- UK: 1kg pork shoulder, 100ml BBQ sauce, 30ml olive oil, salt, pepper, 4 burger buns, coleslaw

Instructions:

1. 1. Preheat your Tefal Easy Fry Air Fryer & Grill to 200°C (390°F).
2. 2. Rub the pork shoulder with olive oil, salt, and pepper.
3. 3. Place the pork shoulder on the grill plate.
4. 4. Grill for 3 hours, turning occasionally and basting with BBQ sauce, until the pork is tender and can be shredded easily.
5. 5. Shred the pork with forks and mix with more BBQ sauce.
6. 6. Serve the pulled pork on burger buns with coleslaw.

Air-Fried Beef and Vegetable Skewers

Prep: 20 mins | Cook: 15 mins | Serves: 4

Ingredients:

- UK: 500g beef sirloin (cubed), 1 red bell pepper (chopped), 1 green bell pepper (chopped), 1 large onion (chopped), 30ml olive oil, 1 tablespoon soy sauce, 1 teaspoon garlic powder, salt, pepper

Instructions:

1. 1. Preheat your Tefal Easy Fry Air Fryer to 200°C (390°F).

2. In a bowl, toss the beef cubes, bell peppers, and onion with olive oil, soy sauce, garlic powder, salt, and pepper.
3. Thread the beef and vegetables onto skewers.
4. Arrange the skewers in the air fryer basket in a single layer.
5. Air fry for 12-15 minutes, turning halfway through, until the beef is cooked to your liking and the vegetables are tender.
6. Serve hot with a side of rice or salad.

Grilled Pork Belly Bites with Honey Soy Glaze

Prep: 15 mins | Cook: 20 mins | Serves: 4

Ingredients:

- ❖ UK: 500g pork belly (cubed), 30ml honey, 30ml soy sauce, 1 teaspoon garlic powder, 1 teaspoon ginger powder, salt, pepper

Instructions:

1. Preheat your Tefal Easy Fry Air Fryer & Grill to 200°C (390°F).
2. In a bowl, mix honey, soy sauce, garlic powder, ginger powder, salt, and pepper.
3. Toss the pork belly cubes in the glaze mixture until well coated.
4. Place the pork belly cubes on the grill plate.
5. Grill for 20 minutes, turning halfway through, until the pork belly is crispy and caramelized.
6. Serve hot as a tasty appetizer or main dish.

CHAPTER 5 SEAFOOD DISHES

Air-Fried Coconut Shrimp with Sweet Chili Sauce

Prep: 15 mins | Cook: 10 mins | Serves: 4

Ingredients:

- UK: 500g large prawns (peeled and deveined), 60g shredded coconut, 60g panko breadcrumbs, 2 large eggs (beaten), 60g plain flour, 1 teaspoon garlic powder, 1 teaspoon salt, 1 teaspoon black pepper, 200ml sweet chili sauce

Instructions:

1. Preheat the Tefal Easy Fry Air Fryer to 180°C (356°F).
2. Prepare three separate bowls: one with flour mixed with garlic powder, salt, and pepper; one with beaten eggs; and one with a mixture of shredded coconut and panko breadcrumbs.
3. Coat each shrimp in the flour mixture, then dip in the egg, and finally coat with the coconut and panko mixture.
4. Place the shrimp in the air fryer basket in a single layer. Use the air frying function and cook for 8-10 minutes until golden and crispy.
5. Serve the shrimp hot with sweet chili sauce on the side for dipping.

Grilled Salmon with Mango Salsa

Prep: 15 mins | Cook: 10 mins | Serves: 4

Ingredients:

- UK: 4 salmon fillets (about 150g each), 1 tablespoon olive oil, salt, pepper, 1 ripe mango (diced), 1 small red onion (diced), 1 red bell pepper (diced), juice of 1 lime, 1 tablespoon fresh coriander (chopped)

Instructions:

1. Preheat the Tefal Easy Fry Grill function to 200°C (392°F).
2. Brush the salmon fillets with olive oil and season with salt and pepper.

3. Place the salmon fillets on the grill plate and cook for about 5 minutes on each side or until the fish flakes easily with a fork.
4. In a bowl, combine the diced mango, red onion, bell pepper, lime juice, and cilantro/coriander to make the salsa.
5. Serve the grilled salmon topped with the fresh mango salsa.

Air-Fried Fish Tacos with Cabbage Slaw

Prep: 20 mins | Cook: 12 mins | Serves: 4

Ingredients:

- UK: 500g white fish fillets (such as cod or tilapia), 60g panko breadcrumbs, 2 large eggs (beaten), 60g plain flour, 1 teaspoon cumin, 1 teaspoon paprika, salt, pepper, 8 small tortillas, 200g shredded cabbage, 1 carrot (grated), 60ml mayonnaise, juice of 1 lime

Instructions:

1. Preheat the Tefal Easy Fry Air Fryer to 180°C (356°F).
2. Mix the flour with cumin, paprika, salt, and pepper in a bowl. Place the beaten eggs in another bowl and panko breadcrumbs in a third bowl.
3. Coat each fish fillet in the flour mixture, then dip in the egg, and finally coat with the panko breadcrumbs.
4. Place the fish fillets in the air fryer basket. Use the air frying function and cook for 10-12 minutes until crispy and cooked through.
5. Prepare the slaw by mixing shredded cabbage, grated carrot, mayonnaise, and lime juice in a bowl.
6. Warm the tortillas in a pan or microwave.
7. Assemble the tacos by placing pieces of air-fried fish on each tortilla and topping with the cabbage slaw.

Grilled Shrimp Skewers with Garlic Butter

Prep: 20mins | Cook: 8mins | Serves: 4

Ingredients:

- UK: 500g large prawns (peeled and deveined), 2 tablespoons olive oil, 4 cloves garlic (minced), 60g unsalted butter, juice of 1 lemon, 1 tablespoon fresh parsley (chopped), salt, pepper

Instructions:

1. 1. Preheat the Tefal EasyFry Grill function to 200°C (392°F).
2. 2. In a bowl, toss the shrimp with olive oil, minced garlic, salt, and pepper.
3. 3. Thread the shrimp onto skewers.
4. 4. Grill the shrimp skewers for about 3-4 minutes on each side until pink and opaque.
5. 5. Melt the butter in a small saucepan, add lemon juice, and chopped parsley.
6. 6. Brush the grilled shrimp with the garlic butter sauce and serve immediately.

Air-Fried Crispy Calamari Rings

Prep: 15mins | Cook: 10mins | Serves: 4

Ingredients:

- UK: 500g calamari rings, 60g panko breadcrumbs, 30g cornmeal, 2 large eggs (beaten), 60g plain flour, 1 teaspoon paprika, 1 teaspoon garlic powder, salt, pepper, lemon wedges (for serving)

Instructions:

1. 1. Preheat the Tefal EasyFry AirFryer to 180°C (356°F).
2. 2. In a bowl, mix the flour with paprika, garlic powder, salt, and pepper.
3. 3. Place the beaten eggs in another bowl and the panko breadcrumbs mixed with cornmeal in a third bowl.
4. 4. Coat each calamari ring in the flour mixture, then dip in the egg, and finally coat with the breadcrumb mixture.
5. 5. Place the calamari rings in the air fryer basket. Use the air frying function and cook for 8-10 minutes until golden and crispy.
6. 6. Serve hot with lemon wedges on the side.

Grilled Tuna Steaks with Mediterranean Salsa

Prep: 15 mins | Cook: 10 mins | Serves: 4

Ingredients:

- UK: 4 tuna steaks (about 150g each), 2 tablespoons olive oil, salt, pepper, 1 tomato (diced), 1 small red onion (diced), 1 cucumber (diced), 1 tablespoon capers, juice of 1 lemon, 1 tablespoon fresh basil (chopped)

Instructions:

1. Preheat the Tefal EasyFry Grill function to 200°C (392°F).
2. Brush the tuna steaks with olive oil and season with salt and pepper.
3. Grill the tuna steaks for about 4-5 minutes on each side for medium-rare or until desired doneness.
4. In a bowl, combine the diced tomato, red onion, cucumber, capers, lemon juice, and chopped basil to make the Mediterranean salsa.
5. Serve the grilled tuna steaks topped with the fresh salsa.

Air-Fried Crab Cakes with Remoulade Sauce

Prep: 20 mins | Cook: 12 mins | Serves: 4

Ingredients:

- UK: 400g crabmeat, 60g panko breadcrumbs, 1 egg, 60g mayonnaise, 1 tablespoon Dijon mustard, 1 tablespoon lemon juice, 1 teaspoon Old Bay seasoning, 2 tablespoons fresh parsley (chopped), 60g plain flour, 200ml remoulade sauce

Instructions:

1. Preheat the Tefal EasyFry Air Fryer to 180°C (356°F).
2. In a bowl, combine crabmeat, panko breadcrumbs, egg, mayonnaise, Dijon mustard, lemon juice, Old Bay seasoning, and chopped parsley.
3. Form the mixture into small patties and coat each patty lightly with flour.

4. Place the crab cakes in the air fryer basket. Use the air frying function and cook for 10-12 minutes until golden and crispy.
5. Serve the crab cakes hot with remoulade sauce on the side.

Grilled Swordfish Skewers with Pineapple Salsa

Prep: 20 mins | Cook: 10 mins | Serves: 4

Ingredients:

- UK: 500g swordfish steaks (cut into cubes), 2 tablespoons olive oil, salt, pepper, 1 pineapple (diced), 1 red bell pepper (diced), 1 small red onion (diced), juice of 1 lime, 1 tablespoon fresh coriander (chopped)

Instructions:

1. Preheat the Tefal Easy Fry Grill function to 200°C (392°F).
2. Toss the swordfish cubes with olive oil, salt, and pepper.
3. Thread the swordfish onto skewers.
4. Grill the swordfish skewers for about 3-4 minutes on each side until cooked through.
5. In a bowl, combine the diced pineapple, red bell pepper, red onion, lime juice, and cilantro/coriander to make the salsa.
6. Serve the swordfish skewers hot, topped with pineapple salsa.

Air-Fried Fish and Chips

Prep: 20 mins | Cook: 25 mins | Serves: 4

Ingredients:

- UK: 500g white fish fillets (such as cod), 60g panko breadcrumbs, 2 large eggs (beaten), 60g plain flour, 1 teaspoon paprika, salt, pepper, 500g potatoes (cut into chips), 2 tablespoons olive oil, 1 lemon (cut into wedges), tartar sauce (for serving)

Instructions:

1. Preheat the Tefal EasyFry Air Fryer to 200°C (392°F).
2. In a bowl, mix the flour with paprika, salt, and pepper.
3. Coat each fish fillet in the flour mixture, then dip in the egg, and finally coat with panko breadcrumbs.
4. Place the fish fillets in the air fryer basket. Use the air frying function and cook for 12-15 minutes until golden and crispy.
5. In a separate bowl, toss the potato chips with olive oil, salt, and pepper.
6. Place the chips in the air fryer basket and cook for 20-25 minutes, shaking halfway through, until golden and crispy.
7. Serve the fish and chips hot with lemon wedges and tartar sauce.

Grilled Lobster Tails with Garlic Butter

Prep: 15mins | Cook: 10mins | Serves: 4

Ingredients:

- UK: 4 lobster tails, 60g unsalted butter, 2 cloves garlic (minced), juice of 1 lemon, 1 tablespoon fresh parsley (chopped), salt, pepper

Instructions:

1. Preheat the Tefal EasyFry Grill function to 200°C (392°F).
2. Using kitchen shears, cut the top of the lobster shells down to the tail, then pull the meat out slightly and place it on top of the shell.
3. In a small saucepan, melt the butter and add minced garlic, lemon juice, and chopped parsley. Season with salt and pepper.
4. Brush the lobster meat with the garlic butter mixture.
5. Grill the lobster tails for about 5-7 minutes until the meat is opaque and cooked through, basting occasionally with more garlic butter.
6. Serve the lobster tails hot with any remaining garlic butter on the side.

CHAPTER 6 VEGETARIAN AND VEGAN DISHES

Air-Fried Falafel with Tahini Sauce

Prep: 15 mins | Cook: 10 mins | Serves: 4

Ingredients:

- UK: 400g canned chickpeas (drained and rinsed), 1 small onion (chopped), 2 cloves garlic (minced), 30g fresh parsley, 30g fresh coriander, 1 teaspoon ground cumin, 1 teaspoon ground coriander, 1 teaspoon baking powder, 60g plain flour, salt, pepper, 30ml olive oil (for brushing), 60ml tahini, 30ml lemon juice, 1 clove garlic (minced), 60ml water

Instructions:

1. Preheat the Tefal Easy Fry Air Fryer to 180°C.
2. Blend chickpeas, onion, garlic, parsley, coriander, cumin, ground coriander, baking powder, and flour in a food processor until smooth. Season with salt and pepper.
3. Shape the mixture into small balls or patties.
4. Brush the falafel with olive oil and place them in the air fryer basket.
5. Air fry for 10 minutes, turning halfway through, until golden and crispy.
6. Mix tahini, lemon juice, garlic, and water to make the tahini sauce.
7. Serve the falafel hot with tahini sauce on the side.

Grilled Portobello Mushroom Burgers with Caramelized Onions

Prep: 20 mins | Cook: 15 mins | Serves: 4

Ingredients:

- UK: 4 large portobello mushrooms, 30ml balsamic vinegar, 30ml olive oil, 1 teaspoon dried thyme, salt, pepper, 2 large onions (sliced), 30g butter, 4 burger buns, lettuce, tomato slices

Instructions:

1. Preheat the Tefal Easy Fry Grill function to 200°C.
2. Marinate the mushrooms in balsamic vinegar, olive oil, thyme, salt, and pepper for 15 minutes.
3. Caramelize the onions in butter over medium heat until golden brown.
4. Grill the mushrooms for 5-7 minutes on each side until tender.
5. Toast the burger buns on the grill for 1-2 minutes.
6. Assemble the burgers with lettuce, tomato, grilled mushrooms, and caramelized onions.
7. Serve immediately.

Air-Fried Tofu Bites with Teriyaki Glaze

Prep: 15 mins | Cook: 15 mins | Serves: 4

Ingredients:

- UK: 400g firm tofu (drained and cubed), 30ml soy sauce, 1 tablespoon sesame oil, 2 tablespoons cornstarch, 60ml teriyaki sauce, 1 tablespoon sesame seeds, 2 spring onions (chopped)

Instructions:

1. Preheat the Tefal Easy Fry Air Fryer to 200°C.
2. Marinate the tofu cubes in soy sauce and sesame oil for 10 minutes.
3. Coat the tofu with cornstarch.
4. Place the tofu in the air fryer basket and cook for 15 minutes, shaking halfway through.
5. Toss the cooked tofu in teriyaki sauce.
6. Sprinkle with sesame seeds and chopped spring onions before serving.

7. Serve hot.

Grilled Veggie Kebabs with Balsamic Marinade

Prep: 20mins | Cook: 10mins | Serves: 4

Ingredients:

- UK: 1 red bell pepper (cut into chunks), 1 yellow bell pepper (cut into chunks), 1 courgette (sliced), 1 red onion (cut into chunks), 100g cherry tomatoes, 30ml balsamic vinegar, 30ml olive oil, 1 teaspoon dried oregano, salt, pepper

Instructions:

1. Preheat the Tefal EasyFry Grill function to 200°C.
2. In a bowl, mix balsamic vinegar, olive oil, oregano, salt, and pepper.
3. Marinate the vegetables in the balsamic mixture for 15 minutes.
4. Thread the vegetables onto skewers.
5. Grill the kebabs for about 10 minutes, turning occasionally, until charred and tender.
6. Serve the veggie kebabs hot.

Air-Fried Cauliflower Steaks with Romesco Sauce

Prep: 20mins | Cook: 25mins | Serves: 4

Ingredients:

- UK: 1 large cauliflower (cut into 4 steaks), 30ml olive oil, 1 teaspoon smoked paprika, salt, pepper, 100g roasted red peppers, 50g almonds, 1 clove garlic, 30ml olive oil, 1 tablespoon red wine vinegar

Instructions:

1. Preheat the Tefal EasyFry Air Fryer to 180°C.
2. Brush cauliflower steaks with olive oil and season with smoked paprika, salt, and pepper.
3. Place the cauliflower in the air fryer basket and cook for 20-25 minutes until tender and golden.
4. Blend roasted red peppers, almonds, garlic, olive oil, and red wine vinegar to make the Romesco sauce.

5. 5. Serve the cauliflower steaks hot, topped with Romesco sauce.

Grilled Eggplant Parmesan

Prep: 15mins | Cook: 15mins | Serves: 4

Ingredients:

- UK: 2 large aubergines (sliced), 30ml olive oil, salt, pepper, 200g marinara sauce, 100g mozzarella cheese (shredded), 50g parmesan cheese (grated), 10g fresh basil leaves

Instructions:

1. 1. Preheat the Tefal Easy Fry Grill function to 200°C.
2. 2. Brush the aubergine slices with olive oil and season with salt and pepper.
3. 3. Grill the aubergine slices for 5-7 minutes on each side until tender.
4. 4. Layer grilled aubergine, marinara sauce, mozzarella, and parmesan cheese in a baking dish.
5. 5. Grill in the air fryer for an additional 5 minutes until the cheese is melted and bubbly.
6. 6. Garnish with fresh basil leaves before serving.
7. 7. Serve hot.

Air-Fried Chickpea Fritters with Tzatziki Sauce

Prep: 15 mins | Cook: 10 mins | Serves: 4

Ingredients:

- UK: 400g canned chickpeas (drained and rinsed), 1 small onion (chopped), 2 cloves garlic (minced), 30g fresh parsley, 30g fresh coriander, 1 teaspoon ground cumin, 1 teaspoon baking powder, 60g plain flour, salt, pepper, 30ml olive oil (for brushing), 200g Greek yogurt, 1 cucumber (grated), 1 clove garlic (minced), 30ml lemon juice

Instructions:

1. Preheat the Tefal Easy Fry Air Fryer to 180°C.
2. Blend chickpeas, onion, garlic, parsley, coriander, cumin, baking powder, and flour in a food processor until smooth. Season with salt and pepper.
3. Shape the mixture into small patties.
4. Brush the patties with olive oil and place them in the air fryer basket.
5. Air fry for 10 minutes, turning halfway through, until golden and crispy.
6. Mix Greek yogurt, grated cucumber, garlic, and lemon juice to make the tzatziki sauce.
7. Serve the fritters hot with tzatziki sauce on the side.

Grilled Stuffed Bell Peppers with Quinoa and Vegetables

Prep: 20 mins | Cook: 20 mins | Serves: 4

Ingredients:

- UK: 4 large bell peppers (tops cut off and seeds removed), 200g cooked quinoa, 100g corn kernels, 100g black beans, 1 small onion (chopped), 2 cloves garlic (minced), 30g fresh coriander (chopped), 1 teaspoon cumin, 1 teaspoon chili powder, salt, pepper, 30ml olive oil, 100g shredded cheese (optional)

Instructions:

1. Preheat the Tefal Easy Fry Grill function to 180°C.
2. In a bowl, mix cooked quinoa, corn, black beans, onion, garlic, coriander, cumin, chili powder, salt, and pepper.
3. Stuff the bell peppers with the quinoa mixture.

4. Brush the stuffed peppers with olive oil.
5. Place the peppers on the grill and cook for 15-20 minutes until tender.
6. Sprinkle with shredded cheese if desired and grill for an additional 5 minutes until melted.
7. Serve hot.

Air-Fried Vegetable Samosas with Mint Chutney

Prep: 30 mins | Cook: 15 mins | Serves: 4

Ingredients:

- UK: 200g potatoes (peeled and diced), 100g peas, 1 small onion (chopped), 2 cloves garlic (minced), 1 teaspoon ginger (grated), 1 teaspoon cumin seeds, 1 teaspoon coriander seeds, 1 teaspoon garam masala, salt, pepper, 8 sheets filo pastry, 30ml vegetable oil, 100g fresh mint, 1 tablespoon lemon juice, 1 tablespoon sugar, 1 green chili, salt

Instructions:

1. Preheat the Tefal Easy Fry Air Fryer to 180°C.
2. Boil the potatoes and peas until tender. Drain and set aside.
3. Sauté onion, garlic, ginger, cumin seeds, and coriander seeds in a little oil until fragrant.
4. Mix in boiled potatoes, peas, garam masala, salt, and pepper.
5. Cut phyllo sheets into strips, place a spoonful of filling at one end, and fold into triangles.
6. Brush the samosas with vegetable oil and place them in the air fryer basket.
7. Air fry for 12-15 minutes until golden and crispy.
8. Blend mint, lemon juice, sugar, green chili, and salt to make mint chutney.
9. Serve the samosas hot with mint chutney.

Grilled Vegan Lentil Burgers

Prep: 20 mins | Cook: 10 mins | Serves: 4

Ingredients:

- UK: 200g cooked lentils, 100g breadcrumbs, 1 small onion (chopped), 2 cloves garlic (minced), 30g fresh parsley (chopped), 1 tablespoon flaxseed meal, 3 tablespoons water, 1 teaspoon cumin, salt, pepper, 30ml olive oil, 4 burger buns, lettuce, tomato slices

Instructions:

1. Preheat the Tefal Easy Fry Grill function to 200°C.
2. In a small bowl, mix flaxseed meal and water and let sit for 5 minutes to thicken.
3. Combine lentils, breadcrumbs, onion, garlic, parsley, flaxseed mixture, cumin, salt, and pepper in a bowl. Mix well.
4. Shape the mixture into 4 patties.
5. Brush the patties with olive oil.
6. Grill the patties for 5 minutes on each side until golden and firm.
7. Toast the burger buns on the grill for 1-2 minutes.
8. Assemble the burgers with lettuce, tomato, and lentil patties.
9. Serve immediately.

CHAPTER 7 SIDE DISHES

Air-Fried Roasted Potatoes with Rosemary and Garlic

Prep: 10 mins | Cook: 25 mins | Serves: 4

Ingredients:

- UK: 500g baby potatoes (halved), 30ml olive oil, 2 cloves garlic (minced), 2 tablespoons fresh rosemary (chopped), salt, pepper

Instructions:

1. Preheat your Tefal Easy Fry Air Fryer to 200°C.
2. In a large bowl, toss the halved baby potatoes with olive oil, minced garlic, chopped rosemary, salt, and pepper until evenly coated.
3. Place the potatoes in the air fryer basket, ensuring they are in a single layer.
4. Air fry for 25 minutes, shaking the basket halfway through the cooking time for even browning.
5. Once golden and crispy, transfer the roasted potatoes to a serving dish.
6. Serve hot and enjoy as a perfect side to any meal.

Grilled Asparagus with Lemon Garlic Butter

Prep: 10 mins | Cook: 10 mins | Serves: 4

Ingredients:

- UK: 500g asparagus (trimmed), 30g butter, 1 clove garlic (minced), 1 tablespoon lemon juice, salt, pepper

Instructions:

1. Preheat your Tefal Easy Fry Grill function to 200°C.
2. In a small saucepan, melt the butter over low heat. Add the minced garlic and cook for 1-2 minutes until fragrant. Stir in the lemon juice.

3. 3. Arrange the asparagus spears on the grill and brush with the lemon garlic butter. Season with salt and pepper.
4. 4. Grill for 10 minutes, turning occasionally, until the asparagus is tender and slightly charred.
5. 5. Transfer to a serving platter and drizzle with any remaining lemon garlic butter.
6. 6. Serve hot as a delicious and healthy side dish.

Air-Fried Zucchini Fries

Prep: 15 mins | Cook: 12 mins | Serves: 4

Ingredients:

- UK: 500g courgette (cut into sticks), 60g breadcrumbs, 30g grated Parmesan cheese, 1 teaspoon garlic powder, 1 teaspoon paprika, 2 eggs (beaten), salt, pepper

Instructions:

1. 1. Preheat your Tefal Easy Fry Air Fryer to 200°C.
2. 2. In a shallow bowl, combine breadcrumbs, grated Parmesan, garlic powder, paprika, salt, and pepper.
3. 3. Dip each zucchini stick into the beaten eggs, then coat with the breadcrumb mixture, pressing lightly to adhere.
4. 4. Place the coated zucchini sticks in the air fryer basket in a single layer.
5. 5. Air fry for 12 minutes, shaking the basket halfway through, until golden and crispy.
6. 6. Serve the zucchini fries hot with your favourite dipping sauce.

Grilled Corn on the Cob with Chili Lime Butter

Prep: 10 mins | Cook: 15 mins | Serves: 4

Ingredients:

- UK: 4 ears of corn (husks removed), 50g butter (softened), 1 teaspoon chili powder, 1 tablespoon lime juice, salt

Instructions:

1. 1. Preheat your Tefal Easy Fry Grill function to 200°C.
2. 2. In a small bowl, mix the softened butter with chili powder, lime juice, and a pinch of salt until well combined.

3. Brush the ears of corn with the chili lime butter.
4. Place the corn on the grill and cook for 15 minutes, turning occasionally, until the corn is tender and charred in spots.
5. Remove from the grill and brush with any remaining chili lime butter.
6. Serve hot, perfect for a summer BBQ.

Air-Fried Sweet Potato Wedges with Chipotle Mayo

Prep: 10 mins | Cook: 20 mins | Serves: 4

Ingredients:

- UK: 500g sweet potatoes (cut into wedges), 30ml olive oil, 1 teaspoon paprika, 1 teaspoon garlic powder, salt, pepper, 120ml mayonnaise, 1 teaspoon chipotle paste, 1 tablespoon lime juice

Instructions:

1. Preheat your Tefal Easy Fry Air Fryer to 200°C.
2. In a large bowl, toss the sweet potato wedges with olive oil, paprika, garlic powder, salt, and pepper until well coated.
3. Place the wedges in the air fryer basket in a single layer.
4. Air fry for 20 minutes, shaking the basket halfway through, until the wedges are crispy and golden.
5. While the wedges are cooking, mix the mayonnaise, chipotle paste, and lime juice in a small bowl to make the chipotle mayo.
6. Serve the sweet potato wedges hot with the chipotle mayo on the side.

Grilled Balsamic Roasted Brussels Sprouts

Prep: 10 mins | Cook: 20 mins | Serves: 4

Ingredients:

- UK: 500g Brussels sprouts (halved), 30ml balsamic vinegar, 30ml olive oil, 1 tablespoon honey, salt, pepper

Instructions:

1. 1. Preheat your Tefal EasyFry Grill function to 200°C.
2. 2. In a large bowl, mix balsamic vinegar, olive oil, honey, salt, and pepper.
3. 3. Toss the halved Brussels sprouts in the balsamic mixture until well coated.
4. 4. Place the Brussels sprouts on the grill in a single layer.
5. 5. Grill for 20 minutes, turning occasionally, until they are tender and caramelized.
6. 6. Transfer to a serving dish and serve hot.

Air-Fried Parmesan Roasted Green Beans

Prep: 10 mins | Cook: 12 mins | Serves: 4

Ingredients:

- UK: 400g green beans (trimmed), 30ml olive oil, 30g grated Parmesan cheese, 1 teaspoon garlic powder, salt, pepper

Instructions:

1. 1. Preheat your Tefal EasyFry Air Fryer to 200°C.
2. 2. In a large bowl, toss the green beans with olive oil, grated Parmesan, garlic powder, salt, and pepper until evenly coated.
3. 3. Place the green beans in the air fryer basket in a single layer.
4. 4. Air fry for 12 minutes, shaking the basket halfway through, until the green beans are crispy and golden.
5. 5. Transfer to a serving dish and serve hot.

Grilled Hasselback Potatoes with Crispy Bacon

Prep: 15 mins | Cook: 25 mins | Serves: 4

Ingredients:

- UK: 4 large potatoes, 30ml olive oil, 4 strips bacon (chopped), 50g grated cheddar cheese, 2 tablespoons sour cream, 2 tablespoons chives (chopped), salt, pepper

Instructions:

1. Preheat your Tefal EasyFry Grill function to 200°C.
2. Slice the potatoes thinly without cutting all the way through to create the hasselback effect.
3. Brush the potatoes with olive oil and season with salt and pepper.
4. Place the potatoes on the grill and cook for 25 minutes.
5. In a small pan, cook the chopped bacon until crispy.
6. Once the potatoes are tender, top with crispy bacon and grated cheddar cheese. Grill for an additional 5 minutes until the cheese is melted.
7. Serve the potatoes topped with sour cream and chopped chives.

Air-Fried Carrot Fries with Honey Mustard Dip

Prep: 10 mins | Cook: 15 mins | Serves: 4

Ingredients:

- UK: 500g carrots (cut into sticks), 30ml olive oil, 1 teaspoon paprika, salt, pepper, 120ml Greek yogurt, 1 tablespoon honey, 1 tablespoon Dijon mustard

Instructions:

1. Preheat your Tefal EasyFry Air Fryer to 200°C.
2. In a large bowl, toss the carrot sticks with olive oil, paprika, salt, and pepper until evenly coated.
3. Place the carrot sticks in the air fryer basket in a single layer.
4. Air fry for 15 minutes, shaking the basket halfway through, until the carrot fries are crispy and golden.
5. While the fries are cooking, mix the Greek yogurt, honey, and Dijon mustard in a small bowl to make the honey mustard dip.
6. Serve the carrot fries hot with the honey mustard dip on the side.

GrilledGarlicButterMushrooms

Prep:10mins|Cook:10mins|Serves:4

Ingredients:

- UK:400gmushrooms(halved),30gbutter,2clovesgarlic(minced),1tablespoonfreshparsley(chopped),salt,pepper

Instructions:

1. 1.PreheatyourTefalEasyFryGrillfunctionto200°C.
2. 2.Inasmallsaucepan,meltthebutteroverlowheat.Addthemincedgarlicandcookfor1-2minutesuntilfragrant.
3. 3.Tossthehalvedmushroomsinthegarlicbutter,thenseasonwithsaltandpepper.
4. 4.Placethemushroomsonthegrillandcookfor10minutes,turningoccasionally,untiltenderandgolden.
5. 5.Transfertoaservingdishandgarnishwithchoppedparsley.
6. 6.Servehotasaflavourfulsidedish.

CHAPTER 8 SANDWICHES AND WRAPS

Air-Fried Chicken Wraps with Tzatziki Sauce

Prep: 15 mins | Cook: 15 mins | Serves: 4

Ingredients:

- UK: 500g chicken breast (cut into strips), 30ml olive oil, 1 teaspoon garlic powder, 1 teaspoon paprika, salt, pepper, 4 large tortillas, 1 cucumber (grated), 200ml Greek yogurt, 1 clove garlic (minced), 1 tablespoon lemon juice, 1 tablespoon fresh dill (chopped)

Instructions:

1. Preheat your Tefal Easy Fry Air Fryer to 200°C.
2. In a bowl, toss the chicken strips with olive oil, garlic powder, paprika, salt, and pepper until well coated.
3. Place the chicken strips in the air fryer basket and air fry for 15 minutes, shaking the basket halfway through, until golden and cooked through.
4. Meanwhile, make the tzatziki sauce by combining the grated cucumber, Greek yogurt, minced garlic, lemon juice, and chopped dill in a bowl. Mix well and season with salt and pepper.
5. Warm the tortillas in a dry pan or microwave.
6. Fill each tortilla with air-fried chicken strips and a generous spoonful of tzatziki sauce.
7. Roll up the wraps, cut in half, and serve immediately.

Grilled Veggie Panini with Pesto Aioli

Prep: 15 mins | Cook: 10 mins | Serves: 4

Ingredients:

- UK: 1 aubergine (sliced), 1 courgette (sliced), 1 red bell pepper (sliced), 1 yellow bell pepper (sliced), 30ml olive oil, salt, pepper, 8 slices ciabatta bread, 100g mozzarella cheese (sliced), 50g pesto, 50g mayonnaise

Instructions:

1. Preheat your Tefal EasyFry Grill function to 200°C.
2. Toss the sliced vegetables in olive oil, salt, and pepper.
3. Grill the vegetables for 10 minutes, turning occasionally, until tender and slightly charred.
4. While the veggies are grilling, mix the pesto and mayonnaise to make the pesto aioli.
5. Spread pesto aioli on each slice of ciabatta bread.
6. Layer the grilled vegetables and mozzarella cheese on four slices of bread, then top with the remaining slices to form sandwiches.
7. Grill the panini for 5 minutes in the Tefal EasyFry until the bread is crispy and the cheese is melted.
8. Serve hot, cut in half if desired.

Air-Fried Falafel Wraps with Tahini Sauce

Prep: 20 mins | Cook: 15 mins | Serves: 4

Ingredients:

- UK: 400g canned chickpeas (drained and rinsed), 1 onion (chopped), 2 cloves garlic (minced), 30g fresh parsley, 30g fresh coriander, 1 teaspoon ground cumin, 1 teaspoon ground coriander, 1 teaspoon baking powder, 30g flour, salt, pepper, 4 large wraps, 100g lettuce (shredded), 1 tomato (sliced), 50ml tahini, 1 tablespoon lemon juice, 1 tablespoon olive oil

Instructions:

1. Preheat your Tefal EasyFry Air Fryer to 200°C.
2. In a food processor, combine chickpeas, chopped onion, minced garlic, fresh parsley, fresh coriander, ground cumin, ground coriander, baking powder, flour, salt, and pepper. Blend until the mixture is well combined but still slightly chunky.
3. Shape the mixture into small patties and place them in the air fryer basket.
4. Air fry for 15 minutes, shaking the basket halfway through, until the falafel are golden and crispy.
5. Meanwhile, make the tahini sauce by mixing tahini, lemon juice, olive oil, salt, and enough water to reach your desired consistency.
6. Warm the wraps in a dry pan or microwave.
7. Fill each wrap with lettuce, sliced tomato, falafel patties, and a drizzle of tahini sauce.
8. Roll up the wraps, cut in half, and serve immediately.

Grilled Philly Cheesesteak Sandwiches

Prep: 15 mins | Cook: 15 mins | Serves: 4

Ingredients:

- UK: 500g ribeye steak (thinly sliced), 1 onion (sliced), 1 green bell pepper (sliced), 1 red bell pepper (sliced), 30ml olive oil, 8 slices provolone cheese, 4 hoagie rolls, salt, pepper

Instructions:

1. Preheat your Tefal EasyFry Grill function to 200°C.
2. In a bowl, toss the sliced steak, onion, and bell peppers with olive oil, salt, and pepper.
3. Grill the steak and vegetables for 10 minutes, stirring occasionally, until the steak is cooked through and the vegetables are tender.
4. Split the hoagie rolls and place on the grill for 2 minutes to toast.
5. Divide the steak and vegetable mixture among the hoagie rolls and top with slices of provolone cheese.
6. Return to the grill for 3 minutes until the cheese is melted.
7. Serve the Philly cheesesteak sandwiches hot.

Air-Fried BLT Wraps

Prep: 10 mins | Cook: 10 mins | Serves: 4

Ingredients:

- UK: 8 strips bacon, 4 large wraps, 100g lettuce (shredded), 2 tomatoes (sliced), 60ml mayonnaise, 1 avocado (sliced)

Instructions:

1. Preheat your Tefal EasyFry Air Fryer to 200°C.
2. Place the bacon strips in the air fryer basket in a single layer.
3. Air fry for 10 minutes, turning halfway through, until the bacon is crispy.
4. Warm the wraps in a dry pan or microwave.
5. Spread a tablespoon of mayonnaise on each wrap.
6. Layer the lettuce, sliced tomatoes, crispy bacon, and avocado slices on each wrap.
7. Roll up the wraps, cut in half, and serve immediately.

Grilled Caprese Sandwiches

Prep: 10 mins | Cook: 10 mins | Serves: 4

Ingredients:

- UK: 8 slices sourdough bread, 200g fresh mozzarella (sliced), 2 tomatoes (sliced), 30g fresh basil leaves, 30ml balsamic glaze, 30ml olive oil

Instructions:

1. Preheat your Tefal EasyFry Grill function to 200°C.
2. Brush each slice of sourdough bread with olive oil on one side.
3. On the un-oiled side, layer fresh mozzarella slices, tomato slices, and basil leaves.
4. Drizzle with balsamic glaze.
5. Top with another slice of bread, oiled side out.
6. Grill the sandwiches for 5 minutes per side, or until the bread is golden and the cheese is melted.
7. Serve hot, cut in half if desired.

Air-Fried Crispy Tofu Banh Mi Sandwiches

Prep: 20 mins | Cook: 15 mins | Serves: 4

Ingredients:

- UK: 400g firm tofu (sliced), 30ml soy sauce, 1 tablespoon sesame oil, 1 tablespoon rice vinegar, 1 cucumber (sliced), 1 carrot (julienned), 1 daikon radish (julienned), 4 small baguettes, 60ml mayonnaise, 1 tablespoon Sriracha, fresh coriander

Instructions:

1. Preheat your Tefal EasyFry Air Fryer to 200°C.
2. In a bowl, marinate the tofu slices in soy sauce, sesame oil, and rice vinegar for 10 minutes.
3. Place the tofu slices in the air fryer basket in a single layer.
4. Air fry for 15 minutes, turning halfway through, until the tofu is crispy.

5. Mix mayonnaise and Sriracha to make a spicy mayo.
6. Slice the baguettes and spread a layer of spicy mayo on each side.
7. Fill with crispy tofu, cucumber slices, carrot, daikon radish, and fresh coriander.
8. Serve immediately, cut in half if desired.

Grilled Chicken Caesar Wraps

Prep: 15mins | Cook: 15mins | Serves: 4

Ingredients:

- UK: 500g chicken breast (sliced), 30ml olive oil, salt, pepper, 4 large wraps, 100g romaine lettuce (chopped), 50g Parmesan cheese (grated), 60ml Caesar dressing

Instructions:

1. Preheat your Tefal EasyFry Grill function to 200°C.
2. Toss the chicken slices with olive oil, salt, and pepper.
3. Grill the chicken for 10-12 minutes, turning occasionally, until cooked through and golden.
4. Warm the wraps in a dry pan or microwave.
5. Fill each wrap with chopped romaine lettuce, grilled chicken, grated Parmesan, and a drizzle of Caesar dressing.
6. Roll up the wraps, cut in half, and serve immediately.

Air-Fried Buffalo Chicken Wraps

Prep: 10mins | Cook: 15mins | Serves: 4

Ingredients:

- UK: 500g chicken breast (cut into strips), 30ml olive oil, 60ml buffalo sauce, 4 large wraps, 100g lettuce (shredded), 1 carrot (julienned), 50g blue cheese (crumbled), 60ml ranch dressing

Instructions:

1. Preheat your Tefal EasyFry Air Fryer to 200°C.

2. Toss the chicken strips with olive oil and buffalo sauce.
3. Place the chicken strips in the air fryer basket and air fry for 15 minutes, shaking the basket halfway through, until cooked through and slightly crispy.
4. Warm the wraps in a dry pan or microwave.
5. Fill each wrap with shredded lettuce, julienned carrot, buffalo chicken strips, crumbled blue cheese, and a drizzle of ranch dressing.
6. Roll up the wraps, cut in half, and serve immediately.

Grilled Portobello Mushroom Sandwiches

Prep: 10 mins | Cook: 10 mins | Serves: 4

Ingredients:

- UK: 4 large portobello mushrooms, 30ml olive oil, 2 cloves garlic (minced), 4 slices provolone cheese, 4 ciabatta rolls, 100g rocket (arugula), salt, pepper

Instructions:

1. Preheat your Tefal Easy Fry Grill function to 200°C.
2. Brush the portobello mushrooms with olive oil and sprinkle with minced garlic, salt, and pepper.
3. Grill the mushrooms for 10 minutes, turning halfway through, until tender.
4. Split the ciabatta rolls and place on the grill for 2 minutes to toast.
5. Place a slice of provolone cheese on each grilled mushroom.
6. Assemble the sandwiches by layering rocket and the grilled mushrooms on the toasted ciabatta rolls.
7. Serve hot, cut in half if desired.

CHAPTER 9 DESSERTS AND SWEET TREATS

Air-Fried Churros with Chocolate Sauce

Prep: 15mins | Cook: 15mins | Serves: 4

Ingredients:

- UK: 125g plain flour, 240ml water, 60g butter, 1 tablespoon sugar, 1/2 teaspoon salt, 2 large eggs, 50g sugar (for coating), 1 teaspoon cinnamon (for coating), 150g dark chocolate, 120ml double cream

Instructions:

1. Preheat your Tefal EasyFry Air Fryer to 200°C.
2. In a saucepan, bring water, butter, sugar, and salt to a boil. Remove from heat, add flour, and stir until a dough forms.
3. Let the dough cool for a few minutes, then beat in the eggs one at a time until smooth.
4. Transfer the dough to a piping bag fitted with a star tip.
5. Pipe 4-inch strips of dough onto parchment paper.
6. Place the churros in the air fryer basket and air fry for 10-12 minutes until golden brown.
7. Mix sugar and cinnamon in a bowl and roll the hot churros in the mixture.
8. For the chocolate sauce, heat the cream until simmering, then pour over chopped chocolate and stir until smooth.
9. Serve the churros warm with the chocolate sauce for dipping.

Grilled Peaches with Honey Yogurt

Prep: 10mins | Cook: 10mins | Serves: 4

Ingredients:

- UK: 4 peaches (halved and pitted), 30ml olive oil, 240ml Greek yogurt, 2 tablespoons honey, 1 teaspoon vanilla extract, fresh mint leaves (for garnish)

Instructions:

1. Preheat your Tefal EasyFry Grill function to 200°C.
2. Brush the peach halves with olive oil.

3. Grill the peaches for 5 minutes per side until they are tender and have grill marks.
4. In a bowl, mix Greek yogurt, honey, and vanilla extract until well combined.
5. Serve the grilled peaches with a dollop of honey yogurt and garnish with fresh mint leaves.

Air-Fried Apple Fritters

Prep: 15 mins | Cook: 15 mins | Serves: 4

Ingredients:

- UK: 2 apples (peeled, cored, and diced), 125g plain flour, 50g sugar, 1 teaspoon baking powder, 1/2 teaspoon cinnamon, 1/4 teaspoon nutmeg, 1/4 teaspoon salt, 60ml milk, 1 large egg, 1 tablespoon butter (melted), 100g icing sugar, 2 tablespoons milk

Instructions:

1. Preheat your Tefal EasyFry Air Fryer to 200°C.
2. In a bowl, mix flour, sugar, baking powder, cinnamon, nutmeg, and salt.
3. In another bowl, whisk together milk, egg, and melted butter.
4. Combine the wet and dry ingredients, then fold in the diced apples.
5. Drop spoonfuls of batter into the air fryer basket, leaving space between each fritter.
6. Air fry for 10-12 minutes until golden brown, shaking the basket halfway through.
7. Mix icing sugar and milk to make a glaze.
8. Drizzle the glaze over the warm fritters and serve.

Grilled Pineapple Skewers with Coconut Caramel Sauce

Prep: 10 mins | Cook: 10 mins | Serves: 4

Ingredients:

- UK: 1 pineapple (cut into chunks), 30g desiccated coconut, 60ml coconut milk, 100g sugar, 2 tablespoons butter

Instructions:

1. Preheat your Tefal EasyFry Grill function to 200°C.
2. Thread the pineapple chunks onto skewers.
3. Grill the pineapple skewers for 8-10 minutes, turning occasionally, until caramelised and slightly charred.
4. In a saucepan, heat sugar until it melts and turns golden brown.
5. Add butter and coconut milk, stirring until smooth.
6. Stir in desiccated coconut.
7. Serve the grilled pineapple skewers with the coconut caramel sauce.

Air-Fried Baked Apples with Cinnamon and Walnuts

Prep: 10 mins | Cook: 20 mins | Serves: 4

Ingredients:

- UK: 4 apples (cored), 50g walnuts (chopped), 2 tablespoons raisins, 1 tablespoon cinnamon, 2 tablespoons brown sugar, 30g butter (cubed), 120ml apple juice

Instructions:

1. Preheat your Tefal EasyFry Air Fryer to 180°C.
2. In a bowl, mix chopped walnuts, raisins, cinnamon, and brown sugar.
3. Stuff each apple with the mixture and top with a cube of butter.
4. Place the stuffed apples in the air fryer basket.
5. Pour apple juice into the basket around the apples.
6. Air fry for 20 minutes until the apples are tender.
7. Serve warm with a scoop of vanilla ice cream if desired.

Grilled Banana Boats with Chocolate and Marshmallows

Prep: 10 mins | Cook: 10 mins | Serves: 4

Ingredients:

- UK: 4 bananas (unpeeled), 60g mini marshmallows, 50g dark chocolate (chopped), 2 tablespoons chopped nuts

Instructions:

1. Preheat your Tefal EasyFry Grill function to 200°C.
2. Make a slit down the centre of each banana, leaving the peel on.
3. Stuff the bananas with mini marshmallows and chopped dark chocolate.
4. Grill the bananas for 8-10 minutes until the chocolate and marshmallows are melted and gooey.
5. Sprinkle with chopped nuts and serve with a spoon.

Air-Fried Donuts with Assorted Glazes

Prep: 20mins | Cook: 15mins | Serves: 4

Ingredients:

- ❖ UK: 250g plain flour, 50g sugar, 1 teaspoon baking powder, 1/2 teaspoon salt, 1 large egg, 120ml milk, 30g butter (melted), 100g icing sugar, 2 tablespoons milk, 1 teaspoon vanilla extract, 2 tablespoons cocoa powder, sprinkles

Instructions:

1. Preheat your Tefal EasyFry Air Fryer to 180°C.
2. In a bowl, mix flour, sugar, baking powder, and salt.
3. In another bowl, whisk together egg, milk, and melted butter.
4. Combine wet and dry ingredients to form a dough.
5. Roll out the dough on a floured surface and cut out donut shapes.
6. Place the donuts in the air fryer basket and air fry for 10-12 minutes until golden.
7. For the glaze, mix icing sugar with milk and vanilla extract. For chocolate glaze, add cocoa powder.
8. Dip the warm donuts in the glaze and decorate with sprinkles.
9. Let the glaze set before serving.

Grilled Strawberry Shortcake Skewers

Prep: 15 mins | Cook: 10 mins | Serves: 4

Ingredients:

- ❖ UK: 250g strawberries (hulled), 4 shortcake biscuits (cubed), 240ml double cream, 2 tablespoons icing sugar, 1 teaspoon vanilla extract

Instructions:

1. Preheat your Tefal Easy Fry Grill function to 200°C.
2. Thread strawberries and shortcake cubes onto skewers.
3. Grill the skewers for 5-7 minutes, turning occasionally, until the shortcake is toasted and strawberries are slightly softened.
4. Whip the double cream with icing sugar and vanilla extract until stiff peaks form.
5. Serve the skewers with a dollop of whipped cream.

Air-Fried Cinnamon Sugar Pretzel Bites

Prep: 20 mins | Cook: 10 mins | Serves: 4

Ingredients:

- ❖ UK: 250g plain flour, 1 tablespoon sugar, 1 teaspoon salt, 1 packet active dry yeast, 120ml warm water, 50g butter (melted), 50g sugar, 1 teaspoon cinnamon

Instructions:

1. Preheat your Tefal Easy Fry Air Fryer to 180°C.
2. In a bowl, combine flour, sugar, salt, and yeast.
3. Add warm water and mix until a dough forms.
4. Knead the dough on a floured surface for 5 minutes until smooth.
5. Roll the dough into small balls to form pretzel bites.
6. Place the pretzel bites in the air fryer basket and air fry for 8-10 minutes until golden brown.
7. In a bowl, mix melted butter, sugar, and cinnamon.

8. 8. Toss the warm pretzel bites in the cinnamon sugar mixture.
9. 9. Serve immediately.

Grilled Coconut Lime Bars

Prep: 15mins | Cook: 15mins | Serves: 4

Ingredients:

- UK: 200g digestive biscuits (crushed), 100g butter (melted), 60g desiccated coconut, 4 limes (zested and juiced), 397g sweetened condensed milk, 2 egg yolks

Instructions:

1. 1. Preheat your Tefal Easy Fry Grill function to 200°C.
2. 2. Mix crushed biscuits, melted butter, and desiccated coconut. Press the mixture into a lined baking tray to form a base.
3. 3. In a bowl, mix lime zest, lime juice, condensed milk, and egg yolks until smooth.
4. 4. Pour the lime mixture over the biscuit base.
5. 5. Grill for 10-15 minutes until set and slightly browned.
6. 6. Let the bars cool completely before cutting into squares.
7. 7. Serve chilled.

CHAPTER 10 BONUS RECIPES AND TIPS

Air-Fried Nachos with Pulled Pork and Guacamole

Prep: 20 mins | Cook: 10 mins | Serves: 4

Ingredients:

- UK: 200g tortilla chips, 200g pulled pork, 100g shredded cheddar cheese, 1 jalapeno (sliced), 100g cherry tomatoes (halved), 1/2 red onion (chopped), 1 avocado (diced), 1 lime (juiced), 2 tablespoons chopped fresh coriander, salt, pepper

Instructions:

1. Preheat your Tefal Easy Fry Air Fryer to 180°C.
2. Arrange tortilla chips on the air fryer basket.
3. Top with pulled pork, shredded cheddar cheese, sliced jalapenos, cherry tomatoes, and chopped red onion.
4. Air fry for 8-10 minutes until the cheese is melted and bubbly.
5. In a bowl, mash diced avocado with lime juice, chopped coriander, salt, and pepper to make guacamole.
6. Serve the air-fried nachos hot with guacamole on the side.

Grilled Pizza with Assorted Toppings

Prep: 15 mins | Cook: 10 mins | Serves: 4

Ingredients:

- UK: 4 mini pizza bases, 200g pizza sauce, 200g shredded mozzarella cheese, assorted toppings (e.g., pepperoni, bell peppers, mushrooms, olives), fresh basil leaves (for garnish)

Instructions:

1. Preheat your Tefal Easy Fry Grill function to 200°C.
2. Spread pizza sauce over each mini pizza base.

3. Sprinkle shredded mozzarella cheese evenly on top.
4. Add assorted toppings of your choice.
5. Grill the pizzas for 8-10 minutes until the cheese is melted and bubbly.
6. Garnish with fresh basil leaves before serving.

Air-Fried Doughnuts with Raspberry Glaze

Prep: 20mins | Cook: 10mins | Serves: 4

Ingredients:

- UK: 250g plain flour, 50g sugar, 1 teaspoon baking powder, 1/2 teaspoon salt, 1/4 teaspoon nutmeg, 120ml milk, 1 large egg, 30g butter (melted), 100g raspberry jam, 100g icing sugar

Instructions:

1. Preheat your Tefal Easy Fry Air Fryer to 180°C.
2. In a bowl, mix flour, sugar, baking powder, salt, and nutmeg.
3. In another bowl, whisk together milk, egg, and melted butter.
4. Combine wet and dry ingredients to form a dough.
5. Roll out the dough and cut out doughnuts using a doughnut cutter.
6. Place the doughnuts in the air fryer basket and air fry for 8-10 minutes until golden brown.
7. Heat raspberry jam in a saucepan until melted.
8. In a bowl, mix melted jam with icing sugar to make a glaze.
9. Dip warm doughnuts into the glaze and let them set before serving.

Grilled Flatbread with Baba Ghanoush and Feta

Prep: 15mins | Cook: 10mins | Serves: 4

Ingredients:

- UK: 4 pieces of flatbread, 200g baba ghanoush, 100g crumbled feta cheese, 1 tablespoon chopped fresh parsley, 1 tablespoon olive oil

Instructions:

1. Preheat your Tefal Easy Fry Grill function to 200°C.
2. Place flatbread on the grill and cook for 2-3 minutes on each side until lightly charred.
3. Spread baba ghanoush evenly over the grilled flatbread.
4. Sprinkle crumbled feta cheese and chopped parsley on top.
5. Drizzle with olive oil before serving.

Air-Fried Crispy Tofu Bites with Sriracha Mayo

Prep: 15mins | Cook: 15mins | Serves: 4

Ingredients:

- UK: 400g firm tofu, 2 tablespoons cornflour, 1 tablespoon soy sauce, 1 teaspoon garlic powder, 1/2 teaspoon smoked paprika, salt, pepper, 2 tablespoons sriracha sauce, 4 tablespoons mayonnaise

Instructions:

1. Preheat your Tefal Easy Fry Air Fryer to 200°C.
2. Cut the tofu into bite-sized cubes and pat them dry with paper towels.
3. In a bowl, toss tofu cubes with cornstarch, soy sauce, garlic powder, smoked paprika, salt, and pepper until evenly coated.
4. Place the tofu cubes in the air fryer basket in a single layer.
5. Air fry for 12-15 minutes until golden and crispy, shaking the basket halfway through.
6. In a small bowl, mix sriracha sauce and mayonnaise to make the dipping sauce.
7. Serve the crispy tofu bites hot with sriracha mayo on the side.

GrilledPanzanellaSaladwithGrilledBread

Prep:20mins|Cook:10mins|Serves:4

Ingredients:

- UK:4slicesofrusticbread,2tablespoonsoliveoil,200gcherrytomatoes(halved),1cucumber(sliced),1/2redonion(thinlysliced),1bellpepper(diced),50gblackolives,2tablespoonscapers,1tablespoonredwinevinegar,2tablespoonschoppedfreshbasil,salt,pepper

Instructions:

1. 1.PreheatyourTefalEasyFryGrillfunctionto200°C.
2. 2.Brushbreadsliceswitholiveoilandgrillfor2-3minutesoneachsideuntiltoasted.
3. 3.Inalargebowl,combinecherrytomatoes,cucumber,redonion,bellpepper,olives,andcapers.
4. 4.Drizzlewithredwinevinegarandremainingoliveoil.
5. 5.Seasonwithsalt,pepper,andchoppedbasil.
6. 6.Teargrilledbreadintochunksandtosswiththesalad.
7. 7.Lettheflavorsmeldfor10minutesbeforeserving.

Air-FriedPotatoSkinswithBaconandCheddar

Prep:20mins|Cook:30mins|Serves:4

Ingredients:

- UK:4largepotatoes,4slicesbacon(cookedandcrumbled),100gshreddedcheddarcheese,2tablespoonschoppedchives,sourcream(forserving)

Instructions:

1. 1.PreheatyourTefalEasyFryAirFryerto200°C.
2. 2.Scrubpotatoesandpatdry.Prickthemwithaforkandmicrowavefor8-10minutesuntiltender.
3. 3.Cutpotatoesinhalfandscoopouttheflesh,leavinga1/4-inchshell.
4. 4.Brushpotatoskinswitholiveoilandairfryfor8-10minutesuntilcrispy.
5. 5.Fillpotatoskinswithcrumbledbaconandshreddedcheddarcheese.

6. Air fry for an additional 5 minutes until the cheese is melted and bubbly.
7. Garnish with chopped chives and serve with sour cream on the side.

Grilled Vegetable Pasta Salad

Prep: 15mins | Cook: 10mins | Serves: 4

Ingredients:

- UK: 200g pasta, 1 zucchini (sliced), 1 yellow squash (sliced), 1 bell pepper (sliced), 1 red onion (sliced), 100g cherry tomatoes (halved), 2 tablespoons olive oil, 2 tablespoons balsamic vinegar, 1 teaspoon Italian seasoning, salt, pepper, 50g crumbled feta cheese, fresh basil (for garnish)

Instructions:

1. Cook pasta according to package instructions. Drain and set aside.
2. Preheat your Tefal Easy Fry Grill function to 200°C.
3. In a bowl, toss sliced zucchini, yellow squash, bell pepper, and red onion with olive oil, balsamic vinegar, Italian seasoning, salt, and pepper.
4. Grill the vegetables for 3-4 minutes on each side until tender and lightly charred.
5. In a large bowl, combine grilled vegetables, cooked pasta, and cherry tomatoes.
6. Toss with crumbled feta cheese and garnish with fresh basil before serving.

Air-Fried Blooming Onion with Dipping Sauce

Prep: 20mins | Cook: 15mins | Serves: 4

Ingredients:

- UK: 1 large onion, 100g plain flour, 1 teaspoon paprika, 1 teaspoon garlic powder, 1 teaspoon salt, 1/2 teaspoon black pepper, 2 eggs, 100ml milk, cooking spray

Instructions:

1. Preheat your Tefal Easy Fry Air Fryer to 180°C.

2. Cut off the top of the onion and peel the skin. Cut vertically from the top towards the root, stopping about 1/2 inch before the bottom.
3. Turn the onion 90 degrees and make another vertical cut, forming quarters. Repeat to make 16 sections.
4. In a bowl, mix flour, paprika, garlic powder, salt, and pepper.
5. In another bowl, whisk eggs and milk.
6. Dip the onion in the flour mixture, then the egg mixture, and back into the flour mixture, ensuring each petal is coated.
7. Place the onion in the air fryer basket, spray with cooking spray, and air fry for 12-15 minutes until golden and crispy.
8. Serve hot with your favorite dipping sauce.

Grilled Fruit Skewers with Honey Lime Glaze

Prep: 15 mins | Cook: 10 mins | Serves: 4

Ingredients:

- UK: Assorted fruits (such as pineapple chunks, strawberries, mango slices, and kiwi slices), 2 tablespoons honey, 1 lime (juiced), 1 tablespoon melted butter, wooden skewers

Instructions:

1. Preheat your Tefal Easy Fry Grill function to 200°C.
2. Thread assorted fruit onto wooden skewers.
3. In a small bowl, mix honey, lime juice, and melted butter to make the glaze.
4. Brush fruit skewers with the honey lime glaze.
5. Grill the fruit skewers for 3-4 minutes on each side until lightly charred.
6. Serve hot as a delicious and refreshing dessert option.

CONCLUSION

As we reach the end of this culinary journey through the world of airfrying and grilling, I can't help but feel a sense of excitement and satisfaction. When first discovered the TefalEasyFryAirFryer&Grill, Iwasskeptical-how could acompactcountertopappliancepossiblyreplicatetheflavorsandtexturesachievedthroughtraditionalfryingandgrilling methods? But as I delved deeper into its capabilities and experimented with the recipes found within these pages, my doubts quickly dissipated.

What beganas a quest for heal their and more convenient cooking options soon evolved into a new found passion fort heart of airfrying and grilling. Each recipe we explored together unlock the world of possibilities, from crispy and indulgent snacks to succulent grilled main sand decadent desserts that defied the notion of "healthy" eating being blander boring.

Throughout this cookbook, we've not only explored a diverse range of delicious and family-friendly recipes but also gained a deeper understanding of the principles and techniques that make airfrying and grilling such a game-changer in the culinary world. We've learned how to harness the power of rapid air circulation and minimal oi l to achieve that coveted crispiness, while a l so mastering the art of direct grilling to infuse our l she swith smoky, charred flavors that tantalize the taste buds.

From crispy chicken wings and juicy burgers toper fectly grilled seafood and indulgent desserts, we've provent l me and again that the TefalEasyFryAirFryer&Grillis capable of delivering restaurant-quality results in the comfort of your own home. But what truly sets this appliance a partis it sversatility- it's not just a tool for making heal their versions of fried favorites, but a multi-functional cooking power house that can tackle a wider angel of culinary task with ease.

As we bid farewell to the pages of this cookbook, I invite you to reflect on the journey we've undertaken together. Perhaps you started out as a skeptic like me, unsure of how a compact appliance could possibly live up to its promises. Or may be you were simply seeking a healthier and more convenient way to enjoy your favorite meals without sacrificing flavor or texture. Regardless of where you began, I hope that you've emerged from this experience with a new found appreciation fort heart of airfrying and grilling, and a deeper understanding of how these techniques can elevate your cooking game.

But beyond the recipes and techniques, I hope that this cookbook has also inspired you to embrace a more mindful and health-conscious approach to cooking and eating. By incorporating the principles of airfrying and grilling into your daily routine, you're not only nourishing your body with nutrient-dense and flavorful meals but also making a conscious choice to prioritize your well-being.

As you continue to explore the world of airfrying and grilling, remember that this is just the beginning. The possibilities are endless, and with a little creativity and experimentation, you can adapt your favorite recipes to suit this innovative cooking method. Don't be afraid to get adventurous sand put your own spin on the dishes you've learned- after all, the true joy of cooking lies in the ability to make it your own.

And if you ever find yourself feeling stuck or in need of inspiration, remember that this cookbook is here to guide you. Whether you're seeking new recipe ideas, tips for troubleshooting, or simply are fresher on the basics, these pages are at reassure trove of knowledge waiting to be explored.

So, as you embark on your next culinary adventure, embrace the power of the TefalEasyFryAirFryer&Grill with confidence and excitement. Let It be your partner in the kitchen, empowering you to create delicious, healthy, and memorable meals that bring joy to you and your loved ones. Remember, good food is not just about nourishing the body- it's about nourishing the soul, and with this cookbook by your side, you have the tools to do just that.

Printed in Great Britain
by Amazon